# AGGRESSIVE
# WHITETAIL HUNTING

## by Greg Miller

## Photography by Greg Miller and Jeff Miller

Published by

 krause
publications

700 E. State Street • Iola, WI  54990-0001


Please call or write for our free catalog of outdoor publications. Our toll-free
number to place an order or obtain a free catalog is 800-258-0929 or please
use our regular business telephone 715-445-2214 for editorial comment
and further information.


Library of Congress Catalog Number: 94-73155
ISBN: 0-87341-336-9

Printed in the United States of America

# Dedication

To Jacob, who will always
be my special "Buck."

# Acknowledgements

I would be remiss if I didn't first thank God for the abilities which I have enjoyed.

The second biggest thank you must go to my wife Geralyn. She has stood by me through good times and bad, never once wavering, always providing me nothing less than her total support. My love and respect for her are immeasurable. Without her, none of this would be possible.

Thanks also to my dad for getting me started in this great sport, and to my mother for her always positive outlook.

And, of course, thanks to all the special friends and hunting partners I've had throughout the years. People such as Russell Thornberry, Paul Gumness, Swede, Dave Hartman, Kevin Shibilski, my brothers Mike and Jim, and others too numerous to mention. I feel blessed for having had the chance to "share a campfire" with each of you.

A very special thank you goes to my brother Jeff, the best hunting partner and friend anyone could ask for. His research, assistance and constant encouragement are a big reason this book has evolved from a dream into a reality.

Finally, I thank those wonderful white-tailed deer. Without them, my life wouldn't be quite the same.

# About The Author

Born in Wisconsin in 1952, Greg Miller started hunting for white-tailed deer with his father in the Northwoods of his home state at the age of 12.

That first hunt convinced Greg that a nine-day season would not satisfy his desire for pursuing such a noble game animal. A few years later, looking to extend his time in the woods, he bought his first hunting bow and a few arrows.

After graduation from high school, Greg was called away from the Wisconsin deer woods for a four-year stint in the military. He saw extended action in Southeast Asia, logging 81 airborne combat missions aboard an EC-47 during the final months of the Vietnam War. When his tour of duty ended in 1974, Greg headed straight back to Wisconsin.

Even more serious in his pursuit of trophy whitetails, Greg continued to sharpen his deer hunting skills during the next 12 years, becoming proficient in taking large white-tailed bucks with bow and gun. Eventually, his wealth of accrued knowledge about hunting for trophy deer prompted him to write several articles on the subject.

Greg's understanding of white-tailed deer and deer behavior has been recognized by many leading experts in the sport. His articles on white-tailed deer hunting now appear regularly in most of the major outdoor publications in North America. In addition to writing, Greg frequently conducts seminars for deer hunters.

Greg lives in west central Wisconsin with his wife Geralyn and their two children, son Jacob and daughter Jessie Lyn.

# Contents

# Introduction

This may come as a surprise to you: *There are no "absolutes" or "guarantees" in the sport of deer hunting.* That statement rings especially true when you decide to limit your efforts solely to the pursuit of mature bucks.

My years of pursuing these magnificent creatures have taught me some important lessons, but one stands out from the rest. Because of their suspicious nature and secretive ways, big white-tailed bucks seldom are a pushover. Only with a tremendous amount of dedication and hard work can I merely see a big buck during the open season. Getting that buck to walk within range of my weapon often requires a great deal more effort.

During the years I was honing my skills as a trophy deer hunter, very little practical information was available concerning the finer points of hunting for mature whitetails. Hence, much of what I learned during those early years was acquired through a sometimes lengthy process of trial and error.

This extreme lack of practical information prompted me to write my first articles about deer hunting. I felt a strong desire to help educate other aspiring trophy hunters on the intricacies of taking mature bucks consistently. It was, and still is, my intent to help people learn more about hunting deer — without the trial and error process I had endured during the formative years of my career.

Much of the information contained in the following pages is the result of personal research. Additional research has been garnered from conversations I've had with some of the top white-tailed deer authorities in the nation. All of the information is based on fact, none of it on speculation.

And I'm convinced this information will help you be a better hunter. It doesn't matter where in North

America you hunt white-tailed deer, and whether your weapon of choice is a bow or gun. If, to the best of your abilities, you use the aggressive tactics and techniques described on the following pages, good things will happen.

# Chapter 1

# The Aggressive Approach

The aggressive approach to hunting for white-tailed deer really is quite simple. And more importantly, in this busy age, being an aggressive deer hunter does not necessarily mean you must spend an enormous amount of time in the woods. The aggressive approach is suited just as well to the two-day-a-week hunter as to the one who hunts seven days a week. I speak from experience.

For many years, my construction job cut heavily into the amount of time I could devote to scouting and hunting. Yet, I enjoyed some of my most successful seasons in those years when I had very little time to spend in the woods.

Knowing I wouldn't get a lot of time to pursue whitetails, I devised a game plan that would allow me to take full advantage of my limited free hours. Whether that free time figured out to be two hours or two days, I spent as much of that time

*The aggressive approach can be a family affair. Here my wife, Geralyn, and son, Jacob, show off one of the many bucks I had taken because of my aggressive approach to the sport. The 10-pointer was harvested during a recent Wisconsin archery season.*

as possible doing something that just might swing the odds in my favor.

Many of the mature bucks I've harvested over the years were taken strictly because of my aggressive approach to the sport. Two bucks in particular come to mind. One was an old, stubhorn brute that I took in the big woods during gun-season several years ago. The other was a monster buck I harvested with archery gear in the farm country near my home.

The hunt for each of the above-mentioned deer was a prime example of the aggressive approach I'm talking about. During the years when those bucks were taken, my construction job was affording me an ever-decreasing amount of free time. The one saving grace I had was that I'd already developed and honed an approach to the sport that allowed me to use to the fullest the time I had. Aggressiveness!

## Aggressive hunting is a year-round attitude

An aggressive attitude is important in all phases of deer hunting, from spring and preseason scouting, to preparation for the season, through the open season itself, and on into the postseason period. I'm convinced that any and all time spent learning more about the bucks I'm hunting is time wisely spent. This has become more and more evident as the years go by.

The open season is not the only time in which I attempt to learn more about the animals I'm pursuing. In fact, that's probably the main reason why so many aspiring trophy deer hunters fall short in their efforts to harvest quality bucks. Simply put, they spend too few hours in the off-season trying to learn more about the animals they're going to be chasing during the open season.

A select few deer hunters have become aware of the importance of spending time in the woods during the off-season. Personally, I consider spring to be one of the most important times of all for deer hunters to be educating themselves, not only about their quarry, but also about the areas they plan on hunting during future seasons.

# The importance of aggressive spring scouting

The greatest benefit of scouting during the spring is the fact that underbrush and foliage are at their lowest levels at this time of year. This will greatly increase your view. In addition, the woods and fields have lain in a kind of suspended animation throughout the winter months. Frequently, rubs and scrapes look nearly as fresh as the day they were made. The same may be said for much of the deer sign you'll find this time of year.

If you're a deer hunter who already has developed an aggressive attitude, you realize that spring is an excellent time not only to explore new country, but also to search out and decipher rub-lines. Following these visual signposts can tell you much about individual bucks, such as where they bed, where they eat and where they walk when going between these two points. Additionally, walking rub-lines in the spring is an excellent way to locate shed antlers. But more on the intricacies of rubs and rub-lines in a later chapter.

One of the keys to consistent success with mature whitetails is learning all you can about the country these animals call home. And there's no better time to do this than during the spring. Walking your selected hunting areas is absolutely the best way to learn the travel routes, food sources and bedding areas most preferred by the bucks in those areas.

To do this, I first select a specific area. Then, armed with a compass and a topographical map of that area, I spend a full day walking and checking out points of interest I've located beforehand on the map. In addition to checking out selected points of interest, I also try to investigate every square inch of the areas I'll be hunting in the future.

I'm convinced walking *all* of my selected hunting areas is so important because it's the *only* way of learning the precise lay of the land - and what exactly is happening on that land. Believe me, there usually are "hidden" features that just don't show up on topographical maps. Usually, the whitetails in that specific area will be relating strongly to those "hidden" features. (Some of my best stand sites are located in such spots.)

I'm amazed at how much such all-day walks tell me about the places I'm going to be hunting. For instance, my spring walks have revealed areas that are conducive to excellent bowhunting possibilities. In contrast, other areas I've found

*An aggressive attitude on spring scouting trips will enable you not only to explore new territory, but also to locate and decipher rub-lines. Additionally, searching near rub-lines is an excellent way to find shed antlers.*

are better suited for slow, sneak-and-peek hunts during the gun season. Surprisingly, only a couple of weekends are required to become so intimately familiar with a great deal of country. And believe me, this familiarity will pay big dividends during the open season.

Again, the point I'm emphasizing here is that you needn't take a lot of time to do some very effective scouting. All it really takes is an aggressive attitude. You can't get it done if your spare time in the spring is spent in front of the TV, in your fishing boat or on the golf course. The two large bucks I mentioned previously were taken as a direct result of very thorough spring scouting. What I learned during my spring walks played a larger role than any other factor in my harvesting those bucks.

Spring also is an excellent time to search for potential stand sites. Because white-tailed bucks are creatures of habit, there's an excellent chance they will frequent certain preferred rubbing and scraping spots every year. Hence, it's a no-brainer that you establish stand sites that allow you take advantage of this behavior. And the best time to select and prepare these stands is in the spring.

There are two reasons why you should be aggressive in searching for and preparing stand sites in the spring. First, no matter how carefully you prepare your stand sites, a certain amount of disturbance always occurs in the immediate area. Better this disturbance takes place in the spring, well in advance of the season, than during the open season itself. Second, having your stands established and ready to go well in advance of the season means you'll have more time to dedicate to hunting. Remember, the more time you can spend actually hunting, the greater your chances for success.

# Aggressive summer scouting

I'm sure many deer hunters consider the hot months of summer best suited for sitting in front of the air conditioner with a "cold one" in hand. Granted, the heat often is unbearable and the bugs nearly intolerable at this time of year. Yet, the mid- to late-summer period is a great time to do some long-range scouting of your favorite hunting areas. But again, it takes an ambitious and aggressive attitude to crawl away from the air conditioner and to sacrifice exposed body parts to the bugs.

*Successful summer scouting doesn't necessarily mean spending a great deal of time outdoors. In fact, locating a buck like this may take only a hour of your time each day.*

Successful summer scouting doesn't necessarily mean spending a lot of time outside. In fact, the majority of your scouting can be done during the last hour or so of daylight. All you'll need to do is observe prime whitetail feeding spots (such as clear-cuts or crop attractants) at long range. This tactic is an excellent way of determining both the quantity and quality of the bucks in your hunting areas.

Yes, summer is the hottest time of year. And it also can be the "buggiest" time. But if you're serious about increasing your success rate, especially with mature whitetails, then it's important to maintain your aggressive attitude through the summer months. What you learn during this period can be extremely important once the hunting season gets under way. This, too, will be highlighted in a later chapter.

# Aggressive preparation

An aggressive attitude is very important as you prepare for the season. (Bowhunters, especially, should be aware of this.) Getting your gear organized well before opening day means you'll spare yourself all that last-minute rushing around so common to non-aggressive hunters. For example, your hunting clothes should be washed in odorless soap, line-dried and stored in plastic bags many days in advance of the opener. Also, every piece of your gear and equipment should be taken out and inspected to make sure it's in perfect working order. But there's another phase of preparation for which I think an aggressive attitude is extremely important.

Each year I converse with many deer hunters who lost out on chances at big bucks simply because they weren't able to hit what they were shooting at. When I question these individuals further, it becomes apparent they took far less than an aggressive approach to practicing with their weapons before the season opened. And in the case of bowhunters, too many of them stopped practicing once the season opened. Isn't it interesting that the same guys who find plenty of time to hunt find very little — if any — time to become proficient with their weapons?

It takes only a slightly aggressive attitude to become a good shot with a bow or gun. Maybe that's why I have difficulty understanding why there still are hunters not even close to being accomplished marksmen with their weapons. With only a few short hours of practice each week, they could achieve the level of proficiency needed to realize their goal.

# Hunting aggressively

For the open deer season, I can't stress enough the importance of having an aggressive attitude toward any amount of time you're afforded to hunt. If you're able to get out for two hours at a time, fine. But if your schedule is going to permit you only a half-hour, don't assume that is too little time to warrant making an effort.

I remember well a white-tailed buck I shot during our archery season a few years ago. After climbing up into my tree stand, I had only enough time to pull up my bow, get an arrow on the string, come to full draw, line up the sight and release. The amount of time that passed, from when I first climbed to my tree stand until that buck walked by, was a whopping 30 seconds! As I said, just because you have little time to spend on a stand is no excuse not to get out and give it a whirl. You just never know...

Also, don't fall into the rut of being one of the "two hours in the morning, two hours in the evening" crowd. If you enjoy the luxury of having a few days to hunt, spend as much time as you can physically endure actually hunting. I'm not saying you have to stay on your stand all day. Rather, start by putting an extra hour or so into your hunt. Although this small bit of added hunting time may not seem like much at the moment, the extra hours will add up significantly by season's end.

My own aggressive approach finds me spending a certain amount of time (usually about three hours) on my stand in the morning. If deer activity has ceased by the end of this time, then I climb down and leave the area. However, I don't head home. Instead, I use the midday hours to do some valuable in-season scouting. Basically, I check out some areas I'm not currently hunting--but that I suspect might be harboring a good buck or two. I wait until the midday hours when the deer should be tucked safely within the confines of their bedding areas. Therefore, I usually don't have to worry about spooking deer that might be up and about.

I consider these in-season scouting forays very beneficial because they keep me aware — throughout the season — of exactly what's going on in a number of different areas. If one of these areas should suddenly become "hot", I'll know it almost immediately. For instance, a sudden increase in rubbing or scraping activity might prompt me to dedicate quickly at least part of my hunting time to a specific area. Much of my success with big bucks can be attributed directly to the fact that I knew exactly when to start hunting those deer.

Obviously, it takes an aggressive attitude to stay in touch with exactly what's going on during the open season. You're certainly not going to discover any potentially productive hunting spots if you spend your off-stand time bellied up to the table or taking a midday snooze.

# Aggressive postseason tactics

The fact that the season is closed is no excuse to drop your aggressive attitude either. Quite honestly, the postseason period can be the best time to try and determine exactly how a certain buck was able to give you the slip during the just completed season. Gun hunters especially may find this to be the most beneficial of all periods for figuring out a "problem buck."

Head right back into the woods immediately after the season ends, because the bucks are still in what I call their "survival patterns." This means they're displaying the same habits and using the same travel routes as they did during the open hunting season. Walk as much of the targeted area as possible. As you walk, pinpoint travel routes and locate food sources the bucks used when they were being pressured.

Now that the season is closed, don't be afraid to walk right through any spots you suspect the bucks might be using for their daytime hideouts. In fact, purposely seek out these bedding areas, and then walk right through the heart of each one. What you want to do is jump the bucks you suspect might be hiding out in such spots.

If you're able to jump a deer, keep track of exactly where he runs. Obviously, the route taken is the one the buck prefers to use when feeling threatened. Simply put, it's his preferred escape route. Knowing the exact location of these escape routes can go a long way toward putting you in position to harvest a buck during the next season.

There you have it — different tactics you can employ throughout the year to help increase your chances of taking a trophy whitetail. Amazingly, all that's really necessary to make these tactics pay off is just a bit more aggressive attitude.

The remaining chapters in this book detail specific tactics and techniques I've found effective for taking mature white-tailed bucks. But first, a bit of warning: Each and every one of these tactics and techniques is dependent, at least in part, on an aggressive attitude. As I said at the beginning of this chapter, being an aggressive deer hunter doesn't necessarily mean you have to spend hundreds of hours per season in the woods. *Being aggressive means spending the free time you have doing all you can to increase your chances for success.* In that regard, I believe *anyone* can adopt an aggressive deer hunting attitude.

*The postseason period is the best time to try and figure out how a big buck was able to give you the slip. Scouting at this time of year also can provide valuable information about favorite buck bedding areas and preferred escape routes.*

# Chapter 2

# Transition Tactics

In my opinion, no book on hunting white-tailed deer is complete unless at least part of that book deals with hunting during the early fall or transition period. Why do I feel this way? Because I've found this particular phase is the toughest in which to try and harvest a trophy buck.

In most parts of the country, the transition period occurs from mid-September to mid-October. For many of us, this time frame encompasses a great part of the archery season for deer. And if a poll were taken, I'm sure we'd find that hunter success rates for this time are lower than during any other part of the season.

## Why the transition baffles hunters

There are several distinct reasons for this. To begin with, the shy and reclusive behavior displayed naturally by white-tailed bucks makes them tough customers any time. But during the

21

*The highly visible behavior patterns displayed by big bucks during the late summer are quickly abandoned when the transition period arrives.*

early fall/transition period, this problem is compounded by the fact that the bucks so severely restrict their travels. To make matters worse, the majority of this restricted travel takes place under the cover of darkness.But there's another reason why this is such a difficult time to connect with a trophy buck: ignorance. Simply speaking, many hunters aren't aware of the many changes going on at this time of year. Some of these changes are taking place with the deer themselves, while others are occurring within the deer's environment. Regardless, these changes all work against the hunter and drastically lower the chances for a successful hunt.

Much of the written material available to deer hunters today concentrates almost exclusively on hunting during the different phases of the rut, with the pre-rut and the rut itself receiving the most attention. This is because most writers and other authorities on white-tailed deer are well-informed on the fine points of hunting for trophy whitetails during the pre-rut and rut periods. However, few of those same individuals know much about effectively hunting the transition period. Consequently, very little information has been published on this particular subject.

In fact, prior to an article I wrote on the transition period for a national magazine several years ago, I had seen nothing of substance written on the subject. Actually, there's still very little being published about this perplexing time of year.

But this is understandable. Most deer hunters totally ignore this part of the season. They don't hunt or scout at this time, and they make no attempt to gain an understanding of what is happening. As a result, darned few are people are qualified to properly answer the many questions about the early fall/transition period.

Personally, I refuse to sacrifice *any* part of the season simply because I don't understand what's going on. It always has been my first instinct to view such things as a challenge. Also, it has always been my intent to learn all I can about any aspect of hunting for white-tailed deer.

I refer to this time of year as the transition period because transition best describes what is taking place. Both the deer herd and the environment in which the deer live are undergoing major changes at this time. The whitetails are in transition, going from their summer patterns into their fall patterns. The whitetails' environment also is undergoing a transition, as the woods change rapidly from a state of lush, full foliage to a thinned-out state.

Both woods and the deer herd are experiencing major changes at this time of year. The woods rapidly are transforming from their formerly lush state to a thinned-out condition. The whitetails are in transition, shifting from their summer to their fall "lifestyle."

# Why bucks change their behavior

Much of what happens during the transition period, and the resulting negative effects it has on us as deer hunters, can be blamed purely on natural occurrences. To begin with, the seeming carefree and careless attitude displayed by bucks for much of the late summer suddenly disappears. The same animals that were bedding, traveling and feeding together in complete harmony are now starting to get a little less tolerant of each other.

Sparring matches that occurred only on rare occasions and were rather low-key become more frequent and certainly more intense. The subordinate animals take just so much of this aggressive pushing and shoving before moving off in search of an area where they'll be hassled less. This, the breakup of buck bachelor groups, is the first signal of changing times for the deer herd.

The restricted movement pattern (mentioned earlier) displayed by white-tailed bucks during the transition period reflects their need to enter the rut in tip-top shape. In the weeks leading up to the rut the bucks instinctively feed voraciously, while traveling very little.

Of course, this increased food intake and decreased activity means the bucks build up a tremendous amount of body fat. These reserves of body fat play an important role during the upcoming rut, when the bucks may go for days at a time without eating.

Another major disruption occurring this time of year concerns food sources. Foods that whitetails may have been using as a primary source of nutrition throughout much of the late summer will suddenly be ignored. It could be that the foods they've been eating suddenly "go out of season" and lose their appeal to the deer. Or it could be that a new, more preferred food has suddenly become available.

Of course, it's entirely possible that a combination of both of the above-mentioned factors has come into play. I'm convinced that this is the case in most situations. It's not so much that one food has suddenly lost its appeal, as it is that a preferred food has "come into season."

In most parts of the country, the sudden abundance of acorns plays a huge role in whitetails so drastically altering their habits and travel patterns. And in many parts of the upper Midwest, other food sources such as mushrooms and fallen maple leaves can divert deer from previously established

*The breakup of buck bachelor groups is one of the first signals of changing times. Antlered whitetails, once living together in harmony, suddenly become less tolerant of each other.*

*When transition whitetails suddenly go "underground," don't place all the blame on other deer hunters. Small game hunters also can do much to disrupt the daily routines of deer.*

patterns. But whatever the case, rest assured that much of the change taking place amongst the deer herd during the transition is directly attributable to food.

Unbelievably, yet another factor has a great influence on the suddenly shy and reclusive behavior displayed by whitetails during the transition. In many parts of North America, both the archery seasons for deer and small game seasons open at about the same time. This, of course, means that there's a sudden influx of people into the woods and fields.

Areas that have been devoid of human activity for months suddenly can become the focal point for scores of people. Hunters seeking grouse, rabbit and squirrel - although their actions certainly aren't malicious - can do much to drive all the deer in a given area into a strict nocturnal movement pattern. Worse yet, small game hunting may force those deer to seek safety and solitude elsewhere.

After all these negative factors have been brought to light, you may conclude that it's nearly impossible even to see a big buck during the transition period. I'll admit, it can be a tough chore. But impossible? Not hardly!

# How to set up during transition

Setting up as close as possible to buck bedding areas should be your highest priority during the transition period. It also is extremely important to monitor the amount of hunting pressure your selected area is receiving. By talking to landowners, spot-checking roads for parked vehicles and paying attention to deer behavior you can determine if your area is under too much pressure.

However, even after being enlightened about the many negatives present at this time of year and the importance of setting up near bedding areas, many hunters will continue to make the same basic mistakes. But this is understandable.

A great part of the problem lies in what happens just prior to the start of the transition period. In the weeks leading up to the transition, it is common to see bucks of all sizes feeding in open fields during broad daylight. In fact, if ever there is a time when you can actually pattern the daily activity of a mature buck, this is it. (Unfortunately, in most parts of North America, the season is still at least a few weeks away.)

Many hunters, after observing this highly visible behavior during the late summer and early fall, mistakenly assume this

*Transition period "Mistake Number One": positioning a stand at a field edge. Ideally, a stand should be placed as closely as possible to a bedding area.*

behavior will continue into the open season. These individuals then use this as a guideline for determining the proper tactics to employ on opening day. These hunters thus establish stand sites either right in or on the very edge of the food sources. This is the first step in the wrong direction.

By the time bow season opens, buck sightings in those open fields during daylight hours become almost non-existent. That doesn't mean, however, that the bucks have necessarily quit using those fields as a food source. Rather, they've adjusted their schedules to run a slight bit later than in previous weeks. A perfect example of this is illustrated by an experience related to me by my friend, Craig Cousins.

In the weeks leading up to opening day, Craig and hunting partner Todd Sturgul had pinpointed the location of several nice bucks. Each and every evening, long before dark, the group of bachelor whitetails would come out to an alfalfa field to feed. Because of this very obvious pattern, Craig and Todd went ahead and placed their stands right on the edge of the field.

To their disappointment, neither Craig or Todd got a chance at any of the bucks on opening day. In fact, they never even saw an antlered animal during the first five days they hunted. But they did discover what had happened to the bucks.

Craig said afterward, "Just about the time we'd be climbing down from our stands, we'd hear those bucks sparring, rubbing and grunting further back in the woods. Obviously, the bucks were still using the alfalfa as a food source, but they weren't getting to the field until well after dark."

Craig knew it was time for a change in strategy. As he tells it, "I waited until the middle of the day, then followed a runway back away from the field in the direction of the sparring we'd been hearing. I found the perfect tree — situated near to what I thought was the bucks' bedding area — and quickly relocated my stand to that tree. On the first afternoon I sat on the stand, I arrowed the biggest of the bucks we had seen."

This is a perfect example of the behaviors displayed by deer and deer hunters at this time of year. The bucks had been highly visible until just prior to the season opener. Because of this, Craig and Todd had elected to place their stands right on the field edge. Of course, it was the wrong approach, but one that seemed justified by the type of behavior the men had witnessed in previous days.

Hunters who pursue big woods whitetails face an even bigger challenge during the early fall. It's tough enough trying to lay eyes on a big woods buck during the peak of the rut, but trying to get into position to kill one during the transition period can seem impossible.

# Big woods success

To realize any sort of success in big woods during the transition, it's imperative you first do an extensive amount of post-season and spring scouting. This scouting provides an important starting point. Off-season scouting missions can supply the information you'll need to get going in the right direction.

Rub and scrape lines from the previous year are excellent indicators of where the most frequently traveled routes happen to be. Once you've located such bits of sign, determining the exact location of preferred foods and — even more importantly — buck bedding areas will be a much easier task.

Off-season scouting played a huge role in my taking a nice big woods buck during the transition period several years ago. (Admittedly, I initially had located the buck during the previous open season, while on a short, midday scouting mission near a preferred food source.) There was enough buck sign near the food source to tell me that at least one antlered animal was in the vicinity. But my knowledge of the existing time period told me it would be nearly impossible to arrow that buck near the feeding area. Any chance I had lay in finding an ambush point somewhere back away from the food, and nearer his bedding area.

Because I was fairly familiar with this particular tract of land, I needed only a short time to locate and prepare a stand site several hundred yards from the feeding area. Knowing this tract of land the way I did, I knew this spot would put me just a stone's throw from a bedding area.

I gave the area a few days to "cool off" before returning to hunt the stand. Shortly before legal shooting time expired, I detected some movement right on the edge of the bedding area. A few seconds later, a beautiful, high-racked buck walked into view. He dilly-dallied around for a couple minutes before walking by at a mere ten yards. The hit was perfect.

By the time I had recovered the buck, darkness was rapidly closing in. As I started field-dressing my prize, I realized the

*Here's a big woods buck I took during the transition period some years ago. He was shot at last light, just as he exited a bedding area.*

significance of what had just happened. Had I done as many hunters would have and set up near the food, my chances of arrowing that buck would have been nil. It certainly pays to be aggressive!

# Three keys to transition hunting success

As you probably have gathered by now, I've discovered two major keys to realizing some success during the transition period.

First (and foremost): *Become at least slightly familiar with the areas you're hunting.*

Second: *Use that knowledge to try and determine the location of bedding areas.*

Third: *Establish stand sites as close as possible to those bedding areas.*

To make the above principles work, you must know - at all times during the season - exactly what foods are preferred by the deer you're hunting. But this is especially important during the transition period. In addition, you must keep up to date on exactly what foods the deer will be switching to once other preferred foods go "out of season".

For much of the early fall, a white-tailed buck's travel routes will be established in relation to the locations of preferred foods. And it's a fact that your greatest chance for success will be in waiting in ambush along these travel routes. So it only stands to reason that you should become fairly knowledgeable concerning the most preferred whitetail foods in your part of the country.

# An exception to the rule

Although I rarely endorse the technique, there are times when setting up right near a food source can pay off - even during the transition period. But this tactic can be effective only under very select conditions.

The first order of business is locating a preferred food source that's not being disturbed or pressured at all. (This is becoming more difficult every year.) Isolated oak ridges, regrowth areas located back off the beaten path, or "hidden" crop attractants are excellent examples of where you might find such a utopian situation.

In all my years of deer hunting, I've been fortunate enough to find only two places similar to those just described. The first was an oak ridge located in a big woods environment more than a half-mile off the road. The other was a small, but lush alfalfa field located in the farm country near my home. In addition to being some distance from the nearest road, the field was nearly surrounded by woods.

Now, although the habitat type and terrain were extremely different in each situation, the experiences I had in both were identical. Bucks of all sizes continued to use the spots as a primary food source throughout the early part of the archery season.

The major reason I experienced such unbelievable action was due mainly to the fact that I had the areas all to myself. There was no additional hunting pressure of any kind for quite some distance around me. Also, the bedding areas of the bucks lay in close proximity to the food source.

One final bit of advice for aspiring transition period hunters: Learn to recognize and deal with pressure from other hunters. Remember, it's tough enough trying to get a big buck within range during this time of year when it's just you against that deer. But when others move in and create a general disturbance in the area, your chances for success immediately go from slim to none. And whether the disturbance comes from deer hunters or small game hunters, the results will be the same.

When faced with this problem, I've often found it to be in my best interest simply to move on. Although I hate to give up on any area, especially if I know there's a good buck or two around, I often feel it's my only alternative. I just can't effectively hunt deer that are continually being harassed and pressured by others.

I've learned that in order to solve any problem, you first must have a thorough understanding of that problem. If you've read this chapter, I'm confident you now understand the problem - what is happening during the transition period. You're also aware of some specific tactics than can prove effective during this frustrating time. The way I see it, your success rate can only improve.

# Chapter 3

# Pre-Rut Tactics

It's a relief to go from hunting whitetails under the trying conditions of the transition, to hunting under more favorable conditions. The pre-rut period is just such a time. If there is one part of the season in which I think the odds suddenly swing in favor of the hunter, this is it!

What is the pre-rut period? It encompasses the entire time from when velvet shedding begins to the first day does come into estrus (and breeding takes place). But for my purpose, and also for the sake of simplicity, I'll narrow it down a bit. When I refer to the pre-rut, I mean the *two weeks immediately preceding the rut* or breeding period.

As most dedicated deer hunters know, buck behavior undergoes a tremendous transformation during the first stirrings of the pre-rut. The low-key, reclusive days of the transition period are history. From this point forward, white-tailed bucks become more active. To the hunter's benefit, of course, as the pre-rut progresses, this buck activity increasingly takes place during daylight hours.

*Buck activity increases significantly during the pre-rut. To the hunter's benefit, much of this activity takes place during daylight hours.*

During the pre-rut, white-tailed bucks are less food-oriented than they were during transition. Their destinations are dictated more and more by where family groups of deer gather. The pre-rut time also sees the bucks extending their travels somewhat. And they definitely start expending more energy during these travels.

# The magic of the pre-rut

I've fallen in love with this particular time of year. What a great time to be in the woods in the North! The weather has turned bug-killing cool, but hasn't yet developed that finger-numbing, bone-chilling "bite" so common in November. Also, most of the leaves have dropped and the underbrush has died, which greatly increases visibility in the woods. Still, these are not the main reasons I love this time of year so much.

Literally overnight, the woods seem to explode with buck sign. This, my friends, is why I'm so infatuated with the pre-rut time. New rubs and connecting rub-lines appear almost on a daily basis. The same is true of scrapes. Not only do they become more numerous, but the frequency with which they're renewed seems to increase with each passing day.

Obviously, the presence of rubs and scrapes helps to confirm my suspicions about both the quantity and quality of bucks in my hunting areas. But there's another reason why these bits of sign have such a stimulating effect on me - and other deer hunters: At no other time of year do white-tailed bucks relate so strongly to these highly visual signposts.

Because of this relationship, it becomes much easier to locate exactly the routes bucks prefer when moving about their ranges. As anyone even remotely interested in deer hunting understands, being able to predict where a buck will walk can go a long way toward helping us hunters fill our tags.

I've always looked upon this sudden presence of buck sign as a blessing from above. When I as a hunter can eliminate much of the available cover out there and concentrate my efforts on exact spots, my success rate is bound to increase. That's exactly what the presence of rubs and scrapes allows me to do.

*Visual bits of buck sign such as rubs and scrapes allow us to bypass much of the available cover out there and instead concentrate our efforts on exact spots.*

# Taking advantage of rub-lines

Scrapes play a huge role in the daily activities of pre-rut white-tailed bucks. In fact, setting up along active scrape-lines can be an extremely effective tactic at this time of year. (A later chapter is dedicated to scrapes, so at this point I'll focus on other pre-rut tactics and techniques.)

No other fair-chase tactic for hunting trophy whitetails is consistently as productive as setting up along active rub-lines. And at no time is this tactic more effective than during the pre-rut period. I don't make that statement lightly.

I've paid close attention to the various tricks and tactics my hunting partners and I have used to take our bucks over the years. In addition, I've made it a habit when meeting other successful hunters to ask them what specific tactics they have employed on their hunts. From these conversations I've ascertained that the use of rubs and rub-lines is, by far, the most popular and productive white-tailed deer hunting tactic.

If you're not familiar with the term, rub-lines are series of antler rubs found along the preferred travel routes of white-tailed bucks. In most cases, rub-lines will lie between preferred bedding and feeding areas.

As for the length of rub-lines, this seems to differ with each individual buck. In other words, there is no average length. I've seen some rub-lines that were only 200 yards in length, some that twisted and wound for nearly a mile through the woods, and many others that could be described as something in between. Nonetheless, one characteristic was constant - nearly all those rub-lines linked bedding and feeding areas. (The particulars of rub-lines are discussed in a later chapter.)

During the early stages of the pre-rut, it's best to locate your stands away from food attractants and closer to bedding areas. Yes, the bucks have become slightly more active during the early pre-rut, but they haven't thrown caution to the wind. They're still going to display a distinct survivalistic type attitude. In other words, safety is their first and foremost concern.

# Locating your stands during the pre-rut

Basically, I like to start out the pre-rut by placing my stands as close as possible to suspected buck bedding areas. I locate these bedding areas by following rub-lines back from known preferred feeding spots. While following a rub-line, I'm ever mindful of any changes in the topography or terrain that might indicate I'm getting close to a buck's daytime hideout.

Any change in elevation (whether it be a drop or a rise) or in cover (e.g., if the cover suddenly becomes thick and impenetrable), if I begin jumping deer, this could be an indication I'm nearing a bedding area. At such a point, I stop right where I am and look for a suitable ambush point. I then use this stand site as both a hunting location and observation post. Not only is the stand placed to take advantage of any buck movement within range, it's also going to provide me with a way of "spying" on the local deer herd.

As stated before, early pre-rut white-tailed bucks, although noticeably more active than during the transition period, haven't fully abandoned their reclusive lifestyle. Observation, therefore, can be a very valuable hunting aid. Even though my stand may not be exactly in the right spot the first time, information gathered while sitting on that stand eventually can put me in position to harvest a buck.

Often, I've sat on my stand during this particular time period and watched as bucks used covert travel corridors of which, until that moment, I was completely unaware. Most times, this movement has occurred right at last light. But because I was paying attention, I noticed the bucks traveling through the spot. A quick and quiet relocation of my stand has resulted in some of my finest trophy bucks.

Because this observation is so important, a good pair of binoculars are a deer hunter's best friend. This really becomes evident when using a stand as a combination hunting spot/ observation post. Good binoculars let me determine, even under low-light conditions, if the deer that's slipping out of range is a good buck, a so-so buck or maybe even an antlerless animal. I really don't want to relocate my stand unless I'm positive the deer I saw is, indeed, a target animal. The binoculars give me the ability to determine this.

As I said, the early pre-rut bucks don't extend their wanderings into the daylight hours very much. However, this behavior changes drastically in the last week before the first does come into estrus. The bucks become much more active and quite visible during daylight hours. You're just as well served by placing your stands near any concentrated rub sign you locate in and around areas being frequented by family groups of deer.

As you're setting up closer to the family groups, you'll be dealing with a greater number of deer. Does and fawns in

*Late one afternoon, Jeff Miller observed this pre-rut buck using a particular travel corridor some distance away. A quick and quiet relocation of his stand the next day put him in position to harvest the animal.*

these groups are much more apt than the bucks to detect my presence. Therefore, as you set up your stands, try to avoid contact with the antlerless members of the deer herd.

The real beauty of using rubs and rub-lines as a hunting aid during the pre-rut is that, even without seeing the one or more bucks responsible for those rubs, you're able to keep a running tab of each animal's daily activities. This is possible because rub activity increases both in frequency and intensity as the pre-rut progresses.

Notice which runways and travel corridors are showing an increase in rub activity. This will give you an edge when deciding on exact stand placement. And if that rub sign suddenly shifts to another part of the woods, simply relocate your stand to a position that lets you take advantage of the new area of activity.

# Effective calling: less is more

If there's anytime during the season when a mature whitetail might be duped by rattling antlers or a grunt call, that time is the late pre-rut period. One of my favorite tactics entails using a slight bit of calling in conjunction with strategic stand placement along an active rub-line. This strategy has worked well for me a number of times, but one hunt in particular comes to mind.

I had located the beginnings of the rub-line during the first weeks of the archery season. But because most of the buck activity at that time of year was taking place well after dark, I decided against setting up along the rub-line. I did, however, prepare a tree for future stand placement.

A quick spot-check of the area during the last week of October revealed that the rub-line had been worked with much more intensity, and certainly with increased frequency. The time had come to put my plan in motion.

The day was overcast and cool, with just a slight breeze from the northeast. I climbed to my stand, let the area settle down for fifteen minutes, and then went through a rather aggressive, 30-second rattling sequence. As I turned to hang the antlers on a branch behind me, a deep, pig-like grunt broke the stillness of the late-October afternoon.

Immediately, I grabbed my bow, turned my feet to the proper position and stared in the direction from which the grunt had originated. Nearly a half-hour went by before I detected the

*I'm convinced the late pre-rut period is the absolute best time to
dupe a white-tailed buck through calling. However, rattling
and/or grunting should be used very sparingly.*

*A fine 10-point buck I took during the pre-rut. If there is one time when deer hunters enjoy anything resembling an advantage, the pre-rut period is that time.*

slightest flicker of movement. As I watched, a beautiful big-woods buck suddenly appeared on the edge of a thick tamarack swamp 50 yards in front of me.

During the next five minutes the big 10-pointer worked his way into my effective bow range. After another minute of turning this way and that, he finally stepped into the perfect position for my shot. At the hit, the big deer jumped straight into the air, ran 40 yards, then stopped and looked back. He tipped over dead 15 seconds later.

That incident proved to me the effectiveness of both hunting along rub-lines and calling. Nonetheless, I consider calling to be a tactic that should be reserved for very special occasions, and then used only sparingly.

I believe many deer hunters are unsuccessful in their calling efforts because they call too much. Most are under the impression that if a little is good, then a lot has to be that much better. That's just not the way it works.

I've probably had as much success at calling in white-tailed bucks, both by rattling and grunting, as anyone. But this success hasn't come about because I spend so much time blowing on a grunt call or smacking antlers together. The truth be known, I probably spend less time actually calling than most hunters.

Whether using a grunt call or rattling antlers, my pattern remains the same. During a normal three-hour stand session, I'll go through two calling routines. The first routine takes place approximately a half-hour after I'm settled in my stand. The second and final routine takes place about an hour later.

When rattling, I employ a sequence of twisting and grinding that lasts about 30 seconds. The severity of this twisting and grinding is dictated solely by just how far the pre-rut has progressed. For example, in the first week of the pre-rut I do some "tickling" and light sparring with the antlers. But during the second week I use a rattling sequence that's intended to duplicate the sounds of a full-blown buck fight.

If overcalling is the primary reason for failure in rattling or grunting, then calling at the wrong times runs a very close second. After talking to many deer hunters each year, I've concluded that a lot of hunters are totally uneducated in calling whitetails. As a result, these guys are using grunt calls and rattling antlers at a time when the bucks are totally unresponsive to such stimuli. By the time that calling could be productive, the bucks in that area have been thoroughly alerted to the tactic. Again, I stress the point that *all* of my calling efforts are reserved for the two weeks of the pre-rut period.

# Successful use of decoys

Decoying is a relatively new aspect of trophy whitetail hunting that, in recent years, has come on like gangbusters. I have had little opportunity to test these bogus deer, but what little I've seen and heard has me convinced. Decoying, especially when used in conjunction with calling, is one of the most deadly pre-rut tactics available to hunters.

I've had many experiences with mature bucks responding to my calling efforts, only to "hang-up" just out of range. Their behavior made it quite obvious that they knew something wasn't quite right with the whole situation. Eventually, these big deer would turn and move off in the opposite direction — almost as if they knew they'd been had.

I'm sure many who are reading this have witnessed the same thing. The explanation is quite simple. When a white-tailed buck responds to calling, whether it be grunting or rattling, he comes fully expecting to see another buck — or two — already there. But when he arrives at the scene and sees no other deer, he immediately becomes suspicious. Only in a very rare case will a mature white-tailed buck continue to move in for a closer look.

If, however, a decoy has been set up in a position where any responding buck could see it, he likely won't be happy until he's had an up-close look at this "intruder." Provided you keep a low profile and the buck doesn't somehow detect your presence, I believe you eventually will be provided with a shot.

Here's how I think it works. Your calling efforts already have duped the buck into thinking he's heard another buck or two. And when he walks into view, the decoy dupes him into thinking that it was, indeed, another buck he heard. Simply put, your calling has successfully appealed to his sense of hearing. But the visual stimulus provided by the decoy is the final ingredient needed to entice that buck within range.

A few words of warning before incorporating a decoy into your hunting efforts. First, take every precaution to keep the decoy from becoming contaminated with *any* odor that might put a whitetail on guard. Second, place the decoy so the deer you're attempting to dupe doesn't approach from the downwind side of your position. And last, make sure you have a clear shot to the spots you suspect a buck may walk through to check out the decoy.

# Patience and persistence

Despite my confidence about the tactics outlined in this chapter, I don't think it's possible to completely pattern a mature white-tailed buck — even during the pre-rut. Yes, it is possible to learn *where* he's going to walk, but knowing exactly *when* he's going to appear in that spot remains a mystery.

Wild animals aren't caught up in our human, Western emphasis on punctuality. In other words, they don't punch a time clock or plan their activities according to a schedule. And they certainly don't wear a watch.

Patience and persistence, therefore are two of the strongest keys for dealing with trophy whitetails. Without a doubt, this patience and persistence is best invested in sitting along those very obvious bits of sign that appear in such abundance during the pre-rut.

# Chapter 4

# Hunting The Rut

The rut! Is there a deer hunter anywhere who doesn't recognize that three-letter word? And I doubt if any serious deer hunter out there doesn't feel his heart skip a beat at the mere mention of the word. Truly, the rut is a very exciting time of year.

Many deer hunters feel as though they stand their best chance for success during the breeding season. However, although the bucks may, indeed, be much more visible, this doesn't necessarily make them more vulnerable. Strange as it may sound, I believe this high visibility actually makes those big bucks even harder to kill.

## The end of pre-rut patterns

Most of the preceding two to three weeks has been spent hunting along highly visible bits of sign left by the bucks. We've thus been able to pattern the movements of the animals

*Even though big bucks are highly visible during the rut, their unpredictable nature makes them tougher to kill.*

we're hunting. The bucks have been fairly predictable and — if ever there is such a thing — somewhat cooperative. However, once the first does start coming into estrus, forget about trying to ambush a big buck as he travels along a rub-line or freshens a scrape.

Unfortunately, many deer hunters aren't aware of the fact that bucks abandon their patterns when does come into estrus. Those hunters therefore fail, simply because they continue to use pre-rut tactics at a time when such tactics no longer are effective.

I stop using pre-rut tactics the minute I start seeing the first signs of breeding activity. Now, that doesn't mean I abandon my stands near rub-lines and scrapes when I see small, immature bucks chasing does and fawns about the woods. In fact, I don't even consider a change in tactics until I detect the first bit of *mature* buck-doe interaction.

As stated above, I believe the high-visibility of bucks during the rut actually makes them a tougher target. Why do I feel this way? Because once the bucks start becoming more visible, they also become more unpredictable. And once they lose any semblance of predictability, I as a hunter lose an edge I'm seldom afforded.

I'm also convinced that the higher visibility and the general behavior of white-tailed bucks during the rut create another negative factor: many deer hunters take a much more careless approach to their hunting efforts because of the general attitude displayed by rutting bucks. Admittedly, some distinct differences occur amongst the deer during this time frame. But contrary to what many deer hunters might think, these differences do *not* swing the odds in their favor.

For example, a sudden increase in daylight activity doesn't mean the bigger bucks have thrown caution to the wind or have now become stupid. Instead, what's different about this time frame is that bucks are spending most of their time seeking receptive does. Because of this, you must switch your attention to the antlerless members of the species. And any hunting around larger concentrations of deer, especially antlerless animals, drastically decreases your chances of going undetected.

For this very reason, it's imperative you take every precaution to keep your presence a secret. The first order of business is to establish walking routes that allow you to get to and from your stand sites without disturbing the deer in any way. Also, you must strive to keep the resident antlerless deer from "picking you off" when you're occupying a stand.

50

*Whenever you hunt around antlerless deer, your chances of being detected greatly increase. Take every precaution to keep this from happening.*

The number one antagonist of any deer hunter, and the number one ally of whitetails, is the wind. Therefore, be very attentive to wind direction at all times when hunting. But being attentive takes on new meaning when hunting efforts put you in close proximity to larger groups of deer. If you even suspect that wind might compromise the location of a certain stand, select a different spot to hunt.

## Find the family travel routes

Through the years, my hunting partners and I have enjoyed quite a bit of success during the rut by using one tactic in particular. This tactic entails placing our stands along the travel routes that family groups of deer are using to travel between bedding areas and primary food sources.

Because we've come to recognize this as a highly productive tactic during the rut, we try to pinpoint the locations of several different family groups of deer in the days leading up to the breeding period. This information proves highly valuable in that, once breeding begins, we know exactly where to direct our attention. Usually, stand placement is decided only after we've observed deer activity to see which runways are being used the most.

Admittedly, does and fawns during the rut parade by unaccompanied by a buck many more times than they do with a buck. However, we don't let this discourage us. At this time of year, we know it's only a matter of time before a big buck will come tagging along behind an antlerless deer.

## Look for the food

Because their very existence depends on devouring great quantities of highly nutritious foods, it only stands to reason that sources of food are the best places to begin your search for concentrations of antlerless deer. In agricultural regions, alfalfa, corn, soybeans and wheat are sure bet whitetail attractants.

A couple years back, I found the main travel route linking a prime doe/fawn bedding area with a lush alfalfa field. I discovered the well-worn runway during the middle of the pre-rut period. But because buck movement along such corridors is

*Pinpointing the location of family groups of deer in the days leading up to the rut is a must for an aspiring rut-hunter. Once the breeding begins, the bucks will be wherever the does gather.*

rare that time of year, I didn't bother hunting the spot right away.

At the first hint of breeding activity, however, I returned and put up a tree stand overlooking the runway. In a little over a week, I saw eight different bucks while sitting on that stand. The largest, a huge 10 pointer that would have scored almost 150 typical, paraded by me at a mere 15 yards late one morning. A terrible blunder on my part was the only thing that saved the monster buck. Intending to end my hunt for the day, I already had lowered my bow and dropped my tow rope to the ground. I sat unarmed as my lost trophy sauntered away.

Unlike agricultural regions, in big-forest environments food attractants are most often found within the woods. Areas of re-growth stimulated by recent logging action or fires are excel-lent places to search for feeding activity. Also, during years of heavy mast crops (e.g., acorns), stands placed on the edge or even right amongst a group of acorn-laden oaks can be ex-tremely productive. Several seasons ago this tactic placed me in a position to take one of my finest bow and arrow bucks.

I first located and started hunting that big deer during late October. But even though he had been fairly visible through-out the latter stages of the pre-rut period, I was unable to de-termine which rub-line he was going to follow into the stand of oaks.

As expected, the monster buck completely abandoned his rubs and scrapes once the actual breeding began. It seemed whenever I saw him then, he was on the move, either chasing a prospective girlfriend or cruising among the oaks in search of some stray bit of estrus scent.

During subsequent hunts in the area, I began to notice one red oak that seemed to concentrate much of the deer feeding activity. Nearly every antlerless deer that visited the area even-tually ended up directly beneath the oak. What really got my attention, though, was the fact that the buck seemed to cruise within bow range of that oak on nearly every visit to the area.

I soon relocated my tree stand high amidst the branches of the gnarly old red oak. The second time I sat on the stand, the eight-point brute walked within 15 yards of my position. One arrow and a short tracking job later, I was standing over the mature, big-woods buck. His dressed weight was a hefty 217 pounds.

This and other successes have proven to me that hunting correctly at a prime in-woods food source can be a very effec-tive tactic during the peak of the rut. The trick is to pay atten-tion and learn where in that food source the antlerless deer

*I took this hog-bodied buck with my bow during the peak of the rut. The monster deer fell victim to a stand placed near a known doe/fawn feeding area.*

seem to concentrate their feeding activity. This tidbit of information helps me decide exactly where my stand should be placed.

# Get the advantage over cross-trailing bucks

After years of observing bucks during the rut, my partners and I were able to devise another effective tactic that gives us an advantage over these unpredictable creatures. Many times we had sat on our stands and watched rutting white-tailed bucks as they cruised through the woods. It was obvious they weren't walking on any runway or trail. Instead, each buck weaved its way through the woods in that fast-paced "rut-walk," stopping only occasionally to drop its head and sniff the ground. Then it was off again in that same, ground-covering gait.

Many of you who have been out in the woods during the peak of the rut have seen a white-tailed buck display this behavior. But what seems a haphazard jaunt through the woods is, in reality, a very effective method for a rutting buck to thoroughly check out different parts of his range.

Rather than crazily wandering, the buck is traveling through a specific area in a way that allows him to cross as many doe/fawn runways as possible. When he comes to one of these runways, he stops and takes a quick sniff to check for any sweet-smelling does. If he finds nothing that piques his curiosity, he moves on to the next runway. However, if he finds the telltale odor of a doe that's either close to or already in estrus, the buck immediately takes up the trail.

This cross-trailing allows a white-tailed buck to travel about his range, scent-checking for hot does while expending a minimal amount of energy. What we may pass off as an erratic and pointless trip through the woods is, in truth, a naturally endowed and highly effective and efficient method of searching out receptive mates.

But be encouraged. There definitely is a way a hunter can take advantage of the cross-trailing behavior so often displayed by white-tailed bucks during the rut. The method entails knowing the exact locations of several preferred feeding spots for the antlerless deer in a certain locale.

To take advantage of cross-trailing bucks, I strongly recommend placing your stand somewhere along the perimeter of a known food attractant. Experience has shown me that cross-trailing bucks have a propensity for circling and scent-checking the runways that enter and leave a feeding area.

For example, let's suppose the main food attractant is an alfalfa field bordered on three sides by woods. At some point during the day, one or more bucks will walk the three wooded sides of that field and scent-check each and every runway they cross. Of special interest to a hunter is the fact that, usually, those bucks will walk either just inside the woods or right along the very edge of the field. This information is extremely valuable when deciding stand placement.

## Other strategies

Hunting midday hours. It has become apparent to me over the years that a cross-trailing buck is more apt to perform the deed during the late morning and midday hours. The only explanation I have for this is the buck seems to realize that all the antlerless deer will have left the food source by then. By waiting until the midmorning hours, the buck is assured of being able to scent-check every deer that fed in the area.

*Exploiting doe/fawn bedding areas.* There is yet another way of effectively dealing with rutting bucks. Before using this tactic, however, you first must become intimately familiar with the areas in which you're hunting. Simply speaking, this tactic entails establishing stand sites on the edge of, and even right in, doe/fawn bedding areas.

Locating the bedding areas of antlerless deer is best done in the off-season. This also is the best time to locate and prepare stand sites. Trying to locate bedding areas, and to select and prepare stand sites during the open season usually causes too much disruption. Whitetails tolerate very little of this disruption near their daytime sanctuaries.

White-tailed bucks are fully aware that, next to preferred feeding spots, they stand their best chance of finding receptive does in bedding areas. Therefore, it only stands to reason that during the peak of the rut, searching bucks will spend a lot of time in close proximity to bedding areas.

If you're able to situate a stand near or right in a doe bedding area, I strongly recommend getting into that stand before daylight in the morning. If you can accomplish this feat without being detected, then remain on your stand all day. When the

*Hunting right on the edge of doe/fawn bedding areas can be extremely effective during the rut. In order to do it right, however, you must be intimately familiar with any area being hunted.*

rut is in high gear, you can expect to see a buck poking around near that bedding area at sometime during the day.

# Dealing with the pressure of gun season

Most of this chapter has presented tactics that are most effective when hunting with archery equipment. That's mainly because in most parts of the country, gun-deer seasons open after breeding is largely finished. Still, there are those odd years here in Wisconsin (and I suspect other areas as well) when the rut is still going strong during gun season.

But even though breeding is still taking place, most of the tactics I've described won't be very effective. The reason for this is that with the sudden increase in hunting pressure during gun-deer season, the bucks have no choice but to alter their behavior.

Nonetheless, receptive does still are going to be bred. But most survival-conscious bucks are not going to jeopardize their personal safety just to perpetuate the species. It's important to keep this in mind when searching for signs of rutting activity during gun season.

Though you may think otherwise, such areas are not extremely difficult to find. The key signs to look for are places where bucks can find all of the basics, i.e., food, water, cover and does. Lastly, but most importantly, this place must be receiving little or no pressure by other hunters.

No matter where you hunt or how much gun-hunting pressure that area receives, some parcel of land is always overlooked during the season. No doubt, bucks in the vicinity will have found that spot and are carrying on with business as usual.

In years when the rut here in Wisconsin overlaps into the gun-deer season, I almost can guarantee that I'll tag a better than average buck. Surprisingly, most of the places I've found aren't located more than a mile or more from the nearest road. And they aren't found on huge tracts of private land. In fact, most of my best gun season, rut-hunting spots are on public land. More surprisingly, several are a mere stone's throw from some of the busiest roads in the area.

The tactic I employ most often when hunting for rutting bucks during gun season is that of placing tree stands to overlook large expanses of ground. Since my effective range is greatly increased with a firearm, I want to be able see as much area as possible.

Even though the rut still might be going strong, I've found that bucks always decrease activity during gun season. Therefore, the majority of rutting bucks I've shot were taken during the first couple hours in the morning or during the last hour of daylight. Only in rare cases, usually when I've been hunting an area that's received no pressure, have I seen midday rut activity during gun season.

Although I've cited some very effective tactics for hunting during the rut in this chapter, it's important to keep this in mind: white-tailed bucks are never more unpredictable than they are during this time frame. The key to using any of these tactics, therefore, is to be persistent.

Remember, at this time of year an area that seems literally devoid of buck movement one day can be the hub of activity for several different bucks the very next day. The stand that's been totally unproductive for days suddenly can be overrun with bucks. That's just the way it is during the rut.

# Chapter 5

# Curing The Post-Rut Blues

As I stated in the second chapter of this book, I consider the transition period to be the toughest time of all in which to harvest a white-tailed buck. But another time frame ranks right up there on the "difficulty scale" with the transition: the post-rut period.

Again, much of the frustration and low hunter success rates during the post-rut are simply because hunters lack understanding. Adding to this frustration and low success rate is the fact that white-tailed bucks, especially mature animals, once again revert to a reclusive, secretive lifestyle.

Although the pre-rut period and the rut itself are still by far *the* times for optimum buck movement, the post-rut period also can be a good time to catch a buck moving during daylight hours. However, before attempting to hunt a post-rut buck, it's imperative you know exactly what's happening at this time of year.

# Secrets of the post-rut

For about one week after the completion of the rut, white-tailed bucks do very little traveling. It's not unusual for a highly prolific breeding buck to remain in one spot for a few days. A buck feeds very little during this time.

What the bucks are doing is resting up to regain some of the strength and energy they expended during the rigorous days of the rut. Once they've rested enough to recover some strength, they'll start getting "back on their feed" once more.

During my years as a deer hunter, I often have seen a tremendous flurry of activity by white-tailed bucks about a week after the rut has concluded. At the heart of this intense activity is their desire to chow down on highly nutritious foods. Interestingly, big bucks become just as caught up in this intense flurry of activity as smaller bucks.

But what causes this buck behavior I've briefly outlined? During the rut, most white-tailed bucks spend most of their time searching for, chasing and eventually breeding receptive does. This hectic lifestyle often lasts for nearly a month. In that time, the bucks most actively involved in the breeding ritual may lose as much as 30 percent of their body weight.

To avoid entering the winter months with a depleted supply of body fat, the energy-starved bucks then go into a frenzied feeding pattern soon after the rut is completed. In regions where severe winters come roaring in during the latter stages of the rut, prolific breeding bucks are therefore some of the first deer to succumb to the harsh conditions.

White-tailed bucks will be especially feed-active in areas where a sudden cold snap or a major winter storm comes in on the heels of the rut. Such changes in the weather prompt bucks — who had been reclusive and nocturnal — to suddenly abandon their secretive behavior.

Filling their bellies becomes the top priority for energy-sapped bucks. On several occasions when the above-mentioned conditions were present during the post-rut, I've seen huge bucks feeding ravenously in open fields during broad daylight.

My good friend Jim Hole, from Edmonton, Alberta, recently told me that in his area, big bucks really flock to grain and alfalfa fields when the mercury plummets. "This is especially true during the post-rut period in December," Jim observed. "When the temperature gets around the 20 degrees below zero

*White-tailed bucks travel very little in the first week after the rut ends. Instead, they spend most of their time hiding deep within the confines of a secure bedding sanctuary.*

*Post-rut bucks will be most "feed-active" in areas where a sudden cold snap or a major winter storm roars in on the heels of the breeding period. At such a time, it is common to see them up and feeding during daylight hours.*

mark [Fahrenheit], it's not unusual to see huge bucks feeding in the open fields right during midday hours."

Jim also said that, because of the severity of winters at that northern latitude, post-rut bucks have to replenish their exhausted energy supplies as quickly as possible. As you might expect, this pattern remains the same wherever harsh weather conditions occur immediately at the conclusion of the rut.

Of course, it stands to reason that in some parts of the country, post-rut activity will be slightly less pronounced than in other regions. This is especially true in areas where late fall/early winter weather conditions are relatively mild. Still, your best bet for connecting on a buck during the post-rut is to set up somewhere along the corridors he's using to travel between bedding and feeding areas.

Food attractants such as alfalfa, corn, soybeans and wheat can be strong attractants for whitetails found in agricultural areas. In big woods or wilderness environments, look for browse areas (dogwoods, red willow, poplar shoots and young saplings are highly desirable, browse-type foods) and stands of oak that tend to concentrate whitetails. Also, regrowth of any kind always is an attractant.

# Use pre-rut hunting spots during the post-rut

However, being successful during the post-rut period requires more than just knowing the exact locations of preferred whitetail foods. You also must know the exact routes the bucks are taking to reach those foods. More importantly, though, you must pinpoint the locations where those bucks are sleeping away the daylight hours.

If you did even minimal scouting and hunting during the pre-rut period, then you already should be familiar with the locations of the most-used travel routes and preferred daytime hideouts of postseason bucks. Once the rut is finished, whitetailed bucks will return to and take up residence in these home core areas.

An important fact regarding post-rut bucks returning to their core areas: under normal conditions, they will bed in the same spots as before. But to the hunter's advantage is the fact that they start traveling along routes where they feel most safe. This means that the majority of buck movement will, once again, concur with the rub/scrape-lines those deer es-

*Post-rut bucks are notorious for establishing travel routes along the same trails they used most during the pre-rut period. Rub and scrape-lines can reveal exactly where these routes are located.*

tablished earlier during the pre-rut. And not only will post-rut bucks start traveling along their rub/scrape-lines, there's every chance they'll start working those rubs and freshening the scrapes.

Often I've seen evidence of such rubbing/scraping activity during my post-rut hunts in late December here in the Upper Midwest. Of course, the sudden presence of renewed rub/scrape activity is an excellent way to determine exactly which travel corridors post-rut bucks use most often. Setting up along the same rub/scrape-lines that were hunted during the pre-rut period is therefore the most effective tactic during the post-rut. But be warned: merely establishing stand sites anywhere along these routes will not ensure success.

Remember, a combination of factors has driven post-rut bucks deep into seclusion. The most obvious of these factors is the amount of hunting pressure they've experienced in recent weeks. While they aren't fully nocturnal, they have reduced significantly their daylight wanderings. It's therefore best to set up as close as possible to the bedding areas of the bucks you're hunting. Hopefully, you'll have some stand sites from the transition and early pre-rut periods already established in strategic locations. (Yes, these are the exact spots you want to hunt during the post-rut.)

I've found post-rut bucks to be extremely sensitive to any kind of human pressure. So with hunting near bedding areas comes the need to be extremely careful of your conduct when in the woods. This means no unnatural noises, no stray traces of human odor, and no letting your quarry ever lay an eyeball on you.

On occasion, the overwhelming urge to feed can be the Achilles' heel of a post-rut white-tailed buck. When he gets into such a pattern, he seems to throw caution to the wind. This sort of frenzied feeding behavior enabled me to take my biggest bow-killed buck to date.

The weather preceding the momentous day had been relatively warm, especially for December. But according to weather reports, this pattern was about to change. The predictions were for a major winter storm, with heavy snowfall and rapidly falling temperatures.

The approaching storm front caused an unbelievable flurry of deer feeding activity. With nearly a half-hour of legal shooting time remaining, a huge buck walked out of a nearby woods and eased within 15 yards of my stand site.

After several tense minutes, the buck finally offered me a perfect shot angle. As they say, the rest was history. Interest-

*An approaching storm prompted this large non-typical to sacrifice his personal safety for a meal of alfalfa. Happily, I was waiting for just such an opportunity.*

ingly, I had seen three other Pope & Young class bucks in the area before the monster buck made his appearance.

Pronounced buck movement patterns during the post-rut are not something that takes place only in northern latitudes. I witnessed the same type of post-rut movement on two recent hunts in Georgia. At the heart of this movement was the bucks' overwhelming desire to eat.

A good friend, Gary Clancy, joined me on the second of those two Georgia hunts. On the first day alone, Gary saw 43 deer from his stand. Six of those deer were bucks, with one being a real monster. Unfortunately, Gary couldn't get a shot at the big deer. Still, my friend did manage to connect on a dandy nine-pointer. But more impressive than the size of Gary's buck was the fact that he had seen 229 deer in six days of hunting. His total for buck sightings was 27!

My own notes from that same Georgia hunt show that I spotted just over 100 animals. Twelve of these were bucks, of which about half were larger than average. The eight-pointer I shot was the largest of this group.

All the deer that Gary and I saw were traveling back and forth between bedding and feeding areas. This is the exact pattern I've seen post-rut whitetails display here in the North.

# The truth about the "second rut"

You may be wondering why I haven't mentioned the so-called "second-rut" that takes place sometime after the primary breeding period. Honestly, I think far too much has been made of the "second-rut." I believe much of what has appeared in print in recent years about this phenomenon has done more to decrease rather than increase a hunter's chance for success.

After closely monitoring the behavior of wild whitetails for several years, I've concluded that there's no such thing as a pronounced "second-rut." I'd be willing to bet that most experienced deer hunters would agree with me on this.

Unfortunately, too many hunters have been led to believe that an extended flurry of breeding activity takes place during the post-rut. Because of this, they spend valuable time waiting for the "second-rut" to kick into gear.

I will agree that some breeding occurs during what I call the post-rut period. However, the number of antlerless deer coming into estrus is so small, and the times at which they do come into estrus are so staggered, that I've never seen any prolonged rutting activity. In fact, by the time most late-season hunters notice some chasing or breeding, it's too late to take advantage of that action.

Still, because of what they've witnessed and what they've read or heard, such hunters assume the "second-rut" is in full swing. They quickly abandon their stands along known buck travel routes and instead start hunting right amongst the local doe/fawn herds. Obviously, since the rut is underway once more, it's time to employ an effective rut-hunting tactic — right? Wrong.

The rut has not resumed. What has been witnessed is an isolated case of a doe or fawn that, having gone unbred the first time around, has come into estrus once more. That particular estrus cycle is going to last approximately 24 hours, then it's over — and so is the "second-rut."

No doubt a few more antlerless deer in the area also are experiencing another estrus cycle, but it's highly unlikely that many of these unbred deer exist. It's also unlikely they will come into estrus on consecutive days — which really shoots down the possibility of any prolonged "second-rut."

Keep in mind that even though you may witness some definite rut activity during this time of year, you're still far better served sticking by post-rut hunting tactics. 'nuff said.

# Dressing for post-rut weather

By the time white-tailed bucks get into a pronounced post-rut pattern, weather conditions here in the North usually have taken a turn for the worse. So saying, I'd be remiss if I failed to dedicate some space to describing how I dress to deal with the cold temperatures.

Nothing will enable you to deal with the cold like an effective clothes layering system. But using just any type of clothing won't necessarily stop the cold from creeping in. I've found that, when dealing with the cold, it's best to stay away from cotton. Cotton seems to draw warmth away from my body.

For extreme cold-weather hunts, I start with a set of light polypropylene underwear next to my skin. Over this I wear a heavier set of poly. Next comes a set of quilted, thermal underwear. And over the top of these three layers of underwear I wear wool pants and a heavy wool sweater. Over the sweater goes a fleece-lined vest.

*To be an effective postseason hunter, you must dress for the conditions. I recommend a layering system — with the right types of clothing.*

If it's extremely cold, I'll wear one-piece coveralls over the top of everything. But if it's just moderately cold, I'll wear my regular hunting clothes. All my cold weather outer clothing is large enough to keep me from "binding up" when I get all those clothes on underneath. This is extremely important when bow hunting.

On my feet, I start with a light, polypropylene undersock. Over that I wear one or two pairs (depending on the temperature) of heavy, poly/wool blend socks. My boots are pac-types, rated for extremely cold temperatures.

In recent years, I've started using air-activated hand and body warmers when hunting in frigid temperatures. I drop a couple down the back of my shirt, between the two layers of poly underwear, so that they come to rest near my kidneys. I also put a small, hand warmer into the toe of each boot. Lastly, I put one in each of my gloves.

My clothes layering scheme, in combination with the body warmers, has enabled me to remain warm and comfortable on my stand for up to two hours — even when wind chills were pushing the mercury to -60 degrees Fahrenheit. Most importantly, this system allows me to layer up or down according to the temperature.

# Gun hunting in the post-rut

In the previous chapter I mentioned that, occasionally, the rut is still in progress when our gun-deer season opens. Usually, however, rut activity has concluded by the time gun season opens. I believe this is the case in most parts of the country.

Therefore, the tactics described in this chapter are fully applicable during gun season. About the only difference between bow hunting and gun hunting for post-rut bucks involves stand selection. Because a gun's effective range is dramatically longer than that of a bow, exact stand placement isn't such a priority.

There is, however, a tactic that my hunting partners and I have found extremely effective for post-rut, gun season bucks. But that tactic will be explained in a later chapter.

Most hunters of white-tailed deer surely would agree that the best time to kill a buck is during either the late stages of the pre-rut or the during the rut itself. I'm in total agreement with this way of thinking. However, there are times other than those two phases of the rut when quality hunting is possible. With a thorough understanding of what's happening at this time of year, the post-rut period can be one of those times.

Although buck movement certainly isn't on a level with that occurring earlier in the season, it is substantial enough to warrant spending time in the woods. Also, I have found that hunting pressure during the post-rut is just about nonexistent. As far as I'm concerned, that factor alone ensures a quality hunt.

# Chapter 6

# Mastering Small Tracts

My reason for including a chapter on hunting small tracts of land has nothing to do with the fact that such a chapter is easy to write. It also has nothing to do with the fact that I just happen to be well-versed on this subject. It does, however, have everything to do with the decreasing availability of hunting land.

## The case of the disappearing hunting land

Over the past ten years, I've spoken with hundreds of deer hunters. During those same years, I've also been afforded the chance to broaden my own hunting horizons, so to speak. In layman's terms, I've been able to hunt white-tailed deer in many different geographic locations. My many talks with deer hunters, and my own hunts to other states and provinces, have confirmed what I've suspected for several years. The amount of land hunters have available for their efforts is constantly shrinking. Contrary to what you might believe, this isn't a problem unique to your part of the country. In fact, deer hunters everywhere across North America are facing this problem.

Destruction of habitat is one reason for this phenomenon. Farmers and ranchers, looking to increase their "open" acreage, are partly to blame. So are real estate developers who think nothing of turning bulldozers loose on huge tracts of prime whitetail cover.

Urbanization is another culprit. All that "yuppie" housing sprawled across the countryside has meant ever-decreasing hunting lands. Let's face it, few of those people will tolerate deer hunting in their back yards.

But without a doubt, the biggest reason for the shrinkage of available hunting lands is the increasingly popular "No Trespassing" sign. Every year, thousands of acres of prime deer hunting lands suddenly become off-limits to hunters, simply because of the sudden appearance of these all too familiar signs.

Regardless of the reason, hunters everywhere are steadily being forced to stalk deer on smaller and smaller pieces of land. And to consistently realize any kind of success on white-tailed bucks on those small lands, hunters need to have an effective game plan.

And just what is a "small tract"? The answer, of course, may vary from one person to another. However, for the sake of simplicity and as a point of reference, I consider small tracts to be parcels of land ranging from 50 to 500 acres. (But as you'll notice later in this chapter, there are exceptions to this definition.)

# Success in small areas of land

Throughout this chapter I will be emphasizing two words: *observation* and *observe*. This is because, when hunting small tracts of land, a hunter must know exactly what the deer on those lands are doing. And the best way to learn what they are doing is simply to sit back and observe.

*Observation is the key to effectively hunting small tracts of land. And although in-season observations are beneficial, you should start observing during the late summer.*

Late summer is the best time to start observations of any small tracts you'll be hunting. At that time of year, the bucks are in the final weeks of the velvet antlered stage. More importantly, though, even the biggest bucks are highly visible. I've found it common to see huge-racked animals feeding in wide open areas during broad daylight.

For effective observation, take up a vigil some distance away from where you suspect a group of deer may be feeding. Make sure your position prevents your being detected by the deer you're watching. Of course, this means not letting them see, smell or hear you.

Once you've found a good spot from which to fulfil your long-range spying missions, I suggest spending the last hour or two of daylight watching the targeted area. After a week or so, you should have learned much about what's happening on that particular small tract.

You may be wondering how the information compiled at this time of year can be of any benefit later on during the open season. Actually, what you learn during this time frame may well put you in position to harvest a buck.

# The benefits of late summer observation

The first benefit is that there's nothing like a first-hand sighting to confirm that a good buck (or more) is indeed living on the land you'll be hunting. And there's nothing like watching that buck over a period of time for discerning his favorite feeding areas, watering holes and preferred travel corridors.

But how can watching a big buck's behavior in late summer possibly help once the season opens? The answer is relatively simple. During the late summer and early fall, white-tailed bucks spend most of their time within their core areas. Wherever they feed, water and travel this time of year will be the exact same places they'll frequent for much of the fall. (In truth, white-tailed bucks rarely leave their core areas until the latter stages of the pre-rut.)

Clearly, what you learn during late summer observations can provide you the information needed to effectively hunt your small tracts of land. In addition to providing valuable data about both the quantity and quality of bucks, observation helps you determine exactly where your stands should be placed.

*Your late summer and early fall observations should enable you to choose walking routes to your stands that allow you to bypass deer. Such an approach is extremely critical when hunting small tracts of land.*

A second benefit of observing the small tracts of land you'll be hunting has nothing to do with finding out what the bucks are doing. Rather, it has more to do with finding out what the antlerless deer on those tracts of land are doing.

Much of your success on a small tract of land hinges on your ability to move about on that tract of land without being detected by the deer. Therefore you've got to know exactly where the antlerless deer are spending the majority of their time. You can have a stand site established in a spot where you've actually watched a buck walk through on a number of occasions. But if you can't get to that stand site without a bunch of does and fawns snorting and creating a disturbance, you stand a minimal chance of ever killing that buck there.

Your late summer and early fall observations should tell you exactly where the majority of antlerless deer activity is occurring on the small tracts you'll be hunting. With this information in hand, you should then be able to plan walking routes that let you get both to and from your stand sites without incident.

# Stand observation while hunting

My small tract observations continue right into the open season. In fact, I've found some of my best small tract hunting spots by paying attention to what was going on around me while sitting on my stand.

As any other deer hunter, my highest priority when seeking potential stand sites is finding spots that will put me in position to harvest a buck. However, I also want that stand to do double duty as an observation post.

On the stand I pay close attention to everything going on in the area immediately around my stand. In addition, with binoculars I frequently spot-check outlying areas. If I detect any deer activity in an outlying area, I pay close attention to what sort of deer are responsible for that activity.

Quality binoculars are a must here, so I can distinguish if the deer I'm seeing is a big buck, a so-so buck or maybe even antlerless. I want to relocate my stand only if I'm certain doing so will help me take advantage of the big buck's movement patterns. Good binoculars enable me to tell exactly what I'm looking at.

I can't count the number of times this stand observation tactic has enabled me to relocate my stand to a more productive spot. As far as I'm concerned, the strongest evidence that a buck likes to walk through a certain spot is an actual sighting of the buck walking through that spot.

# The importance of spring scouting

I consider spring scouting almost as important as observation while hunting small tracts. On spring scouting missions, I attempt to walk every square foot of every piece of cover on the small tracts I'll be hunting. There's a two-fold purpose for this.

First, walking every square foot of cover helps me locate the "hidden" buck travel corridors that I wouldn't find in any other way. (It's also an excellent way of locating potential stand sites.)

Second, and more importantly, these walks enable me to pinpoint the locations of both doe/fawn and buck bedding areas. Such information is extremely beneficial when hunting a small tract of land. Knowing the location of doe/fawn bedding areas prevent my accidentally stumbling through such areas during the open season. And knowing where the antlered animals prefer to sleep during daylight hours can greatly help in putting me in position to take an early season buck.

# Secrets of preventing area "burn-out"

The biggest problem facing a small tract deer hunter is the danger of completely "burning-out" a piece of property in a relatively short period of time. Only a little human pressure can prompt small tract whitetails to relocate. They can effectively evade your every effort, merely by jumping a fence and taking up residence on adjoining land to which you aren't able to gain access. They still may spend a great deal of time on the farm you're hunting, but most of this activity will take place after dark.

This easily can be caused by what I've come to call the "favorite stand syndrome." Every time they get a chance to hunt, many hunters will occupy one particular stand. They don't care how much time they've spent on the stand in recent days. Worse yet, wind direction has absolutely no bearing on whether or not they'll occupy the stand.

*Very little pressure from hunters can prompt small tract whitetails to move elsewhere. Take every precaution to keep this from happening.*

*This dandy 12-pointer was taken from a small tract by my brother Jeff. Observation during the open season played a large role in Jeff's success.*

Such an approach reduces the chances of success, no matter what sort of terrain you're hunting. And it's an extremely damaging practice when hunting small tracts of land. As I've already mentioned, whitetails that live in such places are the most sensitive of all to human pressure.

Because you stand no chance of filling your tag if a "burnout" pattern develops, it's crucial you take every precaution to keep it from happening. Fortunately, this doesn't entail taking any drastic measures.

My brother Jeff took a fine Pope & Young class buck from a small tract of land a couple years ago. The keys to his success were: (1) continually rotating his hunting efforts, and (2) constant observation of his hunting area.

Jeff first saw the buck from a portable tree stand he had erected in a grove of mature red oaks. The deer in question was with several other "shooter" bucks, but unfortunately for my brother, they all passed by just out of bow range. The antlered caravan continued on their route and exited the woods a short distance away.

Instead of yielding to the temptation to again hunt that stand the very next evening, Jeff elected to sit back and observe the area. Just before dark, he saw the same group of bucks he had seen the evening before. This time, however, they exited the oaks at a different point.

Because of what he had observed, Jeff decided to establish another stand site at this newly discovered exit point. During the first afternoon Jeff sat on this new stand, the biggest of the bucks came walking by at a range of seven yards. At that range, my brother just doesn't miss many shots at big whitetails.

# Secure a variety of small tracts

Many hunters make the mistake of securing permission to hunt only one or two small tracts. This is acceptable only if those one or two tracts have enough space to ensure that hunting won't put too much pressure on the deer living there.

I prefer having access to several small tracts during the season. And on each of those small tracts, I'll establish a number of different stand sites. Such an approach allows me the luxury rotating both my stand sittings and my hunting areas.

Because the subject has such broad appeal, hunting small tracts of land has become a favorite seminar topic of mine.

And after I had finished one such seminar recently, a hunter confronted me with a problem which he had faced.

"I know you said that small tract hunters should establish walking routes that let them get into their stands without alerting the deer — but the tract of land I'm hunting is so small, there's just no way of doing this. You got any suggestions?"

After talking with the guy a bit longer, it soon became apparent his situation was, in truth, hopeless. I finally told him, "I suggest you look for another tract of land to hunt."

"But there are some huge bucks on that land," he countered. "I'd hate to just walk away from it."

"I'm sure you would. But how do you expect to ever get one of those bucks within range if every deer on the property knows not only that you're there, but exactly where you're sitting?" The man finally admitted I was probably right, and decided he'd probably be better served by hunting some different spots.

As I've emphasized before, the top priority of a small tract hunter is keeping a low profile. If you continually run into or disturb deer in any way while going to or from your stand sites, change your walking routes. If this doesn't help, re-evaluate the situation. Your energies might be better spent looking for a new place to hunt.

# Hunting small tracts during the rut

If you have faced something similar to the above-described situations, throughout most of the season your chances for success are just about nil. However, there is a time when you may realize some success.

As many deer hunters know, white-tailed bucks become very nomadic and transient during the rut. This means that, when looking for prospective mates, bucks will put on a lot of miles in a relatively short period of time.

Therefore, when hunting small tracts during the rut, don't be too concerned if you happen to "bump" a deer as you walk to your stand. Things have a way of changing rapidly this time of year. A buck that was a mile or more away when you walked to your stand site may show up right in front of you 30 minutes later.

Because he was a mile away when you were walking to the stand, he likely never heard any deer that might have raised a ruckus about your presence. By the time he comes upon the scene, the area will have had plenty of time to settle down.

# Small tracts in the big woods

Knowing how to effectively hunt small tracts of land can pay off also for people hunting in big woods environments. I've discovered that roughly 90 percent of big woods whitetails spend their time in only about 25 percent of the available cover.

This means that, even though you may be dealing with thousands of acres of cover, you should retain and apply the basic philosophies for effectively hunting small tracts. Believe me, tactics such as establishing covert walking trails to your stand sites and making constant observation are every bit as crucial in the big woods as on small lands.

Once you discover the whereabouts of the home core areas for several big woods bucks, you'll be in pretty good shape. With the exception of the breeding period, these bucks will spend the majority of their time within the boundaries of these core areas.

I think you'll have to agree that it matters little whether the area you're hunting comprises a hundred acres, a thousand acres, or something in between. Having an effective game plan for hunting small tracts of land can serve you well in any environment.

# Chapter 7

# Solving The Big Woods Riddle

As I've already mentioned, the pre-rut period is my favorite time in which to hunt for trophy whitetails. And as you might well imagine, I also have a favorite environment in which I prefer to hunt for such animals. Without a doubt, that environment is the big woods.

As for sheer adversity in the sport of deer hunting, no other environment or habitat comes close to matching the big woods. If I had to cite one reason why I'm so partial to hunting in large tracts of cover, this would be it. I simply love the challenge!

I feel blessed that I was introduced to deer hunting in a big woods environment. Way back in 1950, my dad and 11 other rather serious deer hunters each chipped in $100 to buy a cabin in northwestern Wisconsin. The Stuckert Camp, as it

*Locating and then taking a bragging size buck in the big woods can be a reality. However, it takes more than one or two seasons to learn all there is to know about hunting in such an environment.*

was called, was located smack dab in the middle of some of the largest tracts of roadless cover in that part of the state.

My father took me to this cabin in the big woods in 1964, the first year I was legally old enough to hunt. This was quite an experience for a 12-year-old kid. Never in my life had I been exposed to anything quite like it. Even at such a young age I realized this was a true wilderness

Each night I'd listen to the conversation of the older, more experienced hunters in camp. These talks soon revealed that I could expect to see a wolf or a bear when hunting the big woods. Predictably, this bit of information caused me to spend at least as much time looking over my shoulder as looking ahead. (No wolf or bear was going to sneak up on this novice hunter!)

I spent the next six years hunting with my dad and the other members of the Stuckert Camp. Although I shot a few deer, I never took anything that could be considered "bragging size." Still, I both heard and saw enough to ascertain that some tremendous bucks lived there in the big woods.

Some years later, during our archery season for deer, my real infatuation with big woods whitetails began. Early in the season, I just happened to discover the whereabouts of a tremendous buck. The process took a while, but I eventually was able to modestly pattern the trophy deer. On a cold morning in November, he finally walked within bow range of my stand. There he stood, proof positive that it was entirely possible to single out a particular big woods buck and eventually get into a position to harvest that buck. Admittedly, I was left feeling just a little awed by the enormity of the accomplishment.

Many people have difficulty comprehending the amount of time I've spent honing my skills as a big woods deer hunter. Therein, however, lies my key to consistent success with wilderness whitetails. Believe me, it has taken more than one or two seasons to learn all I need to know about taking mature white-tailed bucks in such an environment.

## Familiarity breeds success

The most common mistake I see aspiring big woods deer hunters making is initially biting off more than they can chew. Too many of these hunters spread their efforts over several different areas, and thus never become intimately familiar with any of those areas.

*Topographical maps can be a great help in searching out new hunting areas. However, such maps are of little use when learning about a specific spot. Walking still is the only way of learning the exact lay of the land.*

I strongly advise aspiring big woods hunters to select a couple of areas and then concentrate *all* their scouting and hunting efforts in those areas. Once a person knows the exact location of every thicket and opening, the precise lay of every ridge and valley, and the spots most preferred by the deer in those areas, then it's time to expand his horizons a bit.

I know from experience that becoming intimately familiar with miles and miles of big woods whitetail habitat can't be accomplished in one or two seasons. And it will never be accomplished unless I'm willing to get off my duff and do some extensive legwork.

As with hunting deer in any environment, there are several tactics and techniques that can prove deadly on big woods whitetails. But in my opinion, the only sure way of attaining an impressive record with mature bucks is by first gaining a thorough knowledge of the terrain in which you're hunting.

By the way, it's all right to use topographical maps as an aid in searching out new country. But don't ever make the mistake of using such maps solely to learn about a specific area. Walking is still the only way to really learn the exact lay of the land.

## Look for the food

I've always found that the best place to start looking for concentrations of deer in a big woods area is near food sources. Locating travel routes and bedding areas becomes significantly more easy once I know exactly where the deer are filling their bellies.

Because agriculture is almost nonexistent in this kind of environment, most of the prime whitetail foods will be found within the woods. So saying then, the most preferred food of big woods deer has been and always will be browse (tender shoots, twigs and leaves). And the best place to search for an abundance of browse is an area currently exhibiting some sort of regrowth.

Despite the efforts of Smokey the Bear, forest fires still are quite common in big woods areas. Although fires always seem devastating as they're burning, they often can prove to be a big woods deer hunter's best friend. I can attest that succulent (to deer) new plant life will be poking through the charred ground only a few weeks after a fire has been extinguished.

Something even more common, and certainly more wide-spread than fire in big woods areas, is logging. Discarded tree-tops left behind by loggers provide instant whitetail food. And the young saplings and bushes that spring up soon after the loggers leave will serve as highly nutritious food sources for several years.

But regardless if it's fire or logging, both of these things stim-ulate immediate regrowth and, as a result, an abundant sup-ply of food. If you're not tuned in to just where you might find such spots in your hunting area, simply contact that county's forestry office.

If no type of regrowth is occurring in the big woods areas you wish to hunt, you'll have to look for other browse-type foods. I've found that big woods whitetails absolutely love sumac, head-high dogwood brush, small maple and poplar shoots, and just about every kind of grass and weed.

Acorns can be another highly sought white-tailed deer food in big woods areas. As many hunters already know, white oak acorns are most preferred by deer, and actually come into sea-son a little earlier than red oak acorns. However, red oak trees are more numerous in most areas and seem usually to pro-duce more acorns. Also, red oak acorns drop over a longer pe-riod of time, so they act as an attractant throughout much of the open deer season.

Keep in mind that oaks are cyclic in their production of acorns. In fact, in most of the big woods areas where I hunt, I count on having a substantial acorn crop only about once ev-ery five years. I therefore check the oaks in my hunting areas in advance of opening day, to determine the presence and abundance of acorns.

Once I've concluded what exactly the deer are eating, I walk the cover around the edges of the food source until I've cir-cumscribed the entire feeding area. I check for buck sign on every runway entering that feeding area. Because I like to limit my pursuits to mature bucks, I pay attention only to those runways with a number of big rubs paralleling their course.

Once I find such sign, I then follow the rubs back away from the food source. By following these rub-lines I'm able to learn a great deal about the preferred travel route of the one or more bucks responsible for the rubs. There's also a good chance a line of rubs may eventually lead me to finding the doorway into a preferred bedding area.

*Locating antler rubs will give you a start on determining the preferred travel routes of big woods bucks. Following rub-lines may enable you to pinpoint both bedding and feeding areas.*

# Spring scouting in the big woods

I like to do the majority of my big woods scouting in the spring. As mentioned in the opening chapter, visibility in the woods increases tremendously at this time of year. Not only does this increased visibility enable me to find scrapes and rubs, it also can assist me in locating certain landmarks throughout the areas I'll be hunting.

Why is locating landmarks important? Because if you know the exact location of a certain ridge, swamp, creek or point of high ground, you'll be able to use that landmark as a reference when navigating the woods. This can be especially important when trying to find your way to and from your big woods stand sites under low light conditions.

As long as existing food sources remain stable (which they generally do in big woods habitat), whitetails will use the same travel routes year after year. Therefore, don't be too concerned if the majority of your information about a specific area was gathered in the spring. There's a very good chance this information will be fully applicable during the next open season.

# Keep walking

Perhaps you're thinking that I overstress the importance of walking to familiarize yourself with the areas you've targeted for future hunting efforts. Perhaps you think it isn't necessary to do all that walking, and that you'll figure out a shortcut to taking big woods bucks. To that I say, "Dream on!"

If you remember and learn only one thing from this chapter, let it be this: Becoming a consistently successful big woods deer hunter is fully dependent on your first adopting the attitude that there's no such thing as walking too much. Personally, I didn't start realizing success with mature, big woods bucks until I'd worn out a couple pairs of boots.

Because of the sheer expanse of the country, big woods environments can intimidate even the most confident deer hunter. If nothing else, therefore, walking will eventually help you overcome this sense of intimidation.

Walking every square foot of the many big woods areas I've hunted also has revealed another fact that's been instrumental in my success. Although they may have miles and miles of cover at their disposal, big woods whitetails use very little of that cover. They eat, drink, bed and breed in very select areas.

*My hunting partners and I pose with a row of big woods bucks taken during a recent season. Such success came about only after we had adopted the attitude that there's no such thing as walking too much!*

And they seldom wander away from those areas - except during the rut.

This means there is far more unproductive than productive country out there. A key to success, then, is being able to quickly identify which areas may have potential and which ones never will. Again, walking will enable you to pinpoint those spots that will provide the best opportunities for taking a big woods buck.

Antler rubs still are the best indicators that a big buck (or more) is dedicating some time to a particular area. And the best place to find rub evidence is along those travel routes that connect bedding and feeding areas.

Only in very rare cases will big woods bucks actually "line out" and take off on a cross-country jaunt. As mentioned previously, this behavior comes about as the result of a breeding urge. Under such conditions, it's nearly impossible to predict exactly where a buck will be or when he'll be there.

For that very reason, a big woods hunter should spend the majority of the season set up along active scrape and rublines. Only when the breeding begins is it time to shift efforts to spots where family groups of deer are known to be feeding.

## Fewer deer can mean a better hunt

I should add that I seldom see many deer on my big woods hunts. In fact, this is a point worth stressing. If you're the type of person who needs to see a large number of deer on every outing, then perhaps you'd better reevaluate your decision to hunt in a big woods environment.

Severe winters and natural predation by bears, wolves, coyotes and bobcats keep the deer herd from ever attaining the kinds of numbers you'll see in agricultural areas. That's just the way it is. But instead of viewing the low deer numbers as a negative factor, I look upon it as a positive thing.

To begin with, any time natural selection is in effect, you're bound to have trophy deer. Severe winters and natural predation continually eliminate the weakest members of the deer herd. The animals that survive to breed and perpetuate the species are the strongest and, as a result, the most apt to achieve trophy status.

As I said, low deer numbers and reduced sightings have never been a deterrent to me when hunting the big woods. (It was something I grew up with.) However, any aspiring big woods

*Low deer densities are the rule rather than the exception in most big woods environments. I prepare myself for this condition by keeping in mind that, if I do see a deer, chances are good that it will be a better than average buck.*

hunter should mentally prepare himself to deal with this condition.

I deal with the mental aspect of big woods hunting by keeping this thought in mind: I may not see a lot of deer, but when I do see one, there's a good chance that deer will be a buck. And I figure the chances are fairly high that the buck will be better than average. So far, I've rarely been disappointed.

There is another advantage to low deer densities. Usually, lower deer numbers mean a tighter buck:doe ratio. Any time such a situation exists, calling becomes much more effective. However, I suggest waiting until the late pre-rut period, as this is the best time to dupe a white-tailed buck with rattling or grunting.

Even though these are big woods areas, it's still possible to use pressure from other gun hunters to your benefit. This exact tactic enabled my brother Mike to harvest 11 white-tailed bucks in as many years.

What's most interesting is that Mike's string of successful seasons didn't take place in many different areas or from several different stand sites. Mike shot every one of those 11 bucks while occupying a stand he had placed 20 feet up in a huge old white pine. The encroachment of hunters from a road nearly a mile south of Mike's stand caused all the bucks from that area to head for a distant patch of thick cover. The old white pine just happened to stand right beside a runway most of the bucks preferred to use en route to that cover.

Locating escape routes is best done during the postseason period. In fact, by referring back to chapter one, you can find out exactly how to go about pinpointing these big woods hot spots.

# Other big woods tactics

Sneaking and peeking is another tactic I greatly enjoy using on my big woods gun hunts. In a way, sneaking and peeking merely is a modified form of still-hunting. Regardless, it's a tactic I seem to be employing more and more these days. But that's only because sneaking and peeking has provided me with chances at a good number of big woods bucks.

For the most part, I like to restrict my sneak and peek hunts to areas with which I'm already familiar. This is because, unlike in still-hunting, I want to move rather briskly through spots where I stand little chance of encountering a buck. I'll then slow down and spend much more time in spots that I think offer a good chance of walking up on a buck.

Another reason for restricting this tactic to familiar areas is because I want to use the lay of the land to my advantage. I have to know the exact location of any small rise or ridge that might increase my visual ability. Also, I have to know exactly which areas the deer will be using at the times of day I'll be hunting them. Most importantly though, I have to know how I can travel about these areas, spying on the deer, while at the same time keeping my own presence secret.

A number of bucks I've taken in the big woods were relating very strongly to old, abandoned home sites. My years of hunting in big woods has shown me that white-tailed bucks show a real affinity for these old home sites. And it's actually quite easy to see why. These places offer the exact things that big bucks love, i.e., food, cover and, in most cases, safe avenues of escape. Also, old home sites seem to draw antlerless deer, which means those spots can really become "hot" once the rut begins.

## Stay invisible

At the beginning of this chapter I wrote of the many challenges associated with hunting for big woods whitetails. One of the biggest of those challenges is the deer themselves. Simply put, their natural wariness and highly suspicious nature creates a natural disadvantage for hunters.

If ever there was a time when you needed to be extremely careful regarding anything and everything associated with being a human, this is it! You must never let the deer you're hunting smell, see or hear you.

I remember well an event during a big woods hunt several years ago that illustrates perfectly the point I'm trying to make. During that hunt I watched three antlerless deer turn tail and run at the sound of a car door being slammed. Interestingly, that car was parked on a road nearly a half-mile away.

If big woods whitetails (and remember, these were antlerless animals) show such sensitivity to a slamming car door, imagine how they'll react to a noseful of human odor or to the sight of a hunter tramping through the woods. Staying invisible is difficult - but extremely important!

In my opinion, chasing mature bucks in the big woods is the epitome of trophy whitetail hunting. Maybe I feel this way because hunting in such an environment has a way of humbling even the most arrogant and cocky people involved in the sport. As far as I'm concerned, it doesn't hurt any of us to occasionally be brought back down to earth.

# Chapter 8

# Speed-Scouting

As with the earlier chapter on hunting small tracts of land, there's a definite reason why I wanted to include a chapter in this book on speed scouting. The ever decreasing amount of land available for hunting isn't the only problem facing today's white-tailed deer hunters. Many of us now are being afforded less and less time to do the things we truly love to do.

## Surviving the "hurry-up" world

Everywhere I go, I'm constantly made aware that more and more people are having to work an increasing number of hours every week just to make ends meet. It's no wonder that we've become such a hurry-up society. We hurry to work in the morning. We hurry to get as much work done as possible during that day. We hurry back home when the workday is over. And when we get back home, it's a mad scramble to see how much "enjoyment" we can cram into that little bit of free time we have left.

Unfortunately, too many people allow their hurry-up attitudes to spill over into their hunting efforts. When the weekend rolls around, these individuals try to cram a week's worth of hunting into Saturday and Sunday. And even though it remains a very important practice during the open season, absolutely no thought is given to scouting. It's simply hunt, hunt, hunt!

# A scouting tactic for hunters with little time

Whether you're one of those who has no extra time for scouting, or whether you're one of those who just doesn't want to spend much time scouting, it doesn't matter. This chapter on speed-scouting is for you. If done properly, speed-scouting can be a highly effective way of learning a great deal about a targeted area — while expending very little time or energy. Speed-scouting, it would seem, is the perfect strategy for our hurry-up society.

For the most part, my job as a construction worker has reduced my hunting time to weekends, just as for everybody else. And as everybody else, I prefer to spend the majority of my free time hunting, not scouting.However, I've discovered that, to be consistently successful with trophy whitetails, it's imperative I keep up to date on what's going on in the areas I'm hunting during the open season. No matter how much I dislike the idea, I have to dedicate at least part of my free time to scouting.

One of the first times I actually applied a bit of speed-scouting to my own efforts resulted in my taking a very good buck with my bow. Of course, this went a long way toward convincing me that success is linked directly to effective scouting. It also convinced me that I didn't necessarily need a lot of time to do some effective scouting.

# How I discovered speed-scouting

In my case, I'd been told by a friend about an area where a good number of deer were feeding in an alfalfa field. Unfortunately, I'd never hunted the area before. To make matters

*Speed-scouting can be a highly effective way of learning a great deal about a specific area - while expending the least amount of time and energy. This technique is perfectly suited to today's "hurry-up" society.*

worse, this place was a good distance "out of my way," so to speak. At best, I'd be reduced to swinging through the area on the drive home from my hunting cabin and doing a short, midday scouting tour. Upon arriving at the spot, the first thing I did was walk all the way around the alfalfa field. On that walk, I stayed right along the edge of the field, just a few yards out from the tree line.

I soon ascertained that, although there was a large amount of buck sign on several different runways entering the field, one runway showed more rub activity than any other. I quickly followed this runway about a quarter-mile back off the field and found even more encouraging sign. Scattered about in a small clearing were about a dozen wrist-sized poplars. Every one of those poplars had been worked over in recent days by an ambitious buck or bucks. As luck would have it, a huge old red oak stood a mere 12 yards from this very obvious staging area. It took only a short time to get my tree stand in place in the oak.

As I drove away, I looked at my watch. I had spent a grand total of 55 minutes scouting the area and selecting a tree for my stand. Admittedly, I felt just a little guilty about not spending more time looking around. But I justified my actions by telling myself that even though I hadn't spent a lot of time scouting, my stand certainly looked to be in the best spot. A week later — and the first time I sat on the stand in the oak - five different bucks walked by me at a range of 12 yards. I never made a move to draw my bow on any of the first four bucks. But the last one, a heavy-bodied 10 pointer, prompted me to act.

I waited until the 10-pointer dropped his head and sniffed the ground. At that point, I came to full draw. I settled my top sight-pin on the lung area of the buck, took a fraction of second to double-check everything, then touched the trigger on my release. The arrow whisked through the 10-pointer and he took off in that head-down charge characteristic of a fatally hit deer. I found the buck after a short, 75-yard tracking job.

As I stood admiring my prize, a thought popped into my mind. I had never hunted this particular area prior to this day. Yet I had spent less than an hour scouting the territory and choosing what proved to be the perfect spot for my stand. After a while I realized that my accomplishment wasn't a fluke.

From the start, I'd known I was pressed for time. This meant I had to get a lot accomplished in a very short time on the day I scouted the spot. So I simply forgot about trying to familiarize

*This 10-point buck was taken during the 1981 archery season.
I spent only 55 minutes scouting the buck.*

myself with every square foot of the area and instead concentrated on finding the spot with the most buck sign.

It doesn't take a genius to see that my speed-scouting approach had worked to perfection on that day many seasons ago. And it has done so on many occasions since. At the heart of ensuring success is knowing how to go about getting the maximum benefit out of a minimal amount of time.

As the above incident with the 10-pointer so vividly proves, speed-scouting isn't a tactic that's effective only in areas with which you're already familiar. If done right, it also can be effective in completely foreign areas.

Normally, I begin by studying topographical maps and then designating specific spots I suspect might warrant a quick, speed-scouting job. For example, any type of funnel that shows up on the map is going to be investigated. The same thing applies to "points" (a narrow section of high ground than juts out into a swamp or other low ground) and also to severe changes in elevation — or "breaks" as I call them.

# Speed-scouting the drainages

Of course, drainages are *always* good places to check for signs of deer activity. And it doesn't matter if that drainage is a river, creek, swamp, beaver marsh, lake or pond. If whitetails are anywhere in the vicinity, they'll be relating strongly to that drainage. In fact, all wild animals relate to drainages. As proof, I offer the following.

The next time you take a trip in your car, pay attention to where most road-killed animals lie. You'll probably see most of these animals, including deer, lying close to where some kind of drainage either crosses or meets the road.

Whitetails love to use creeks and rivers as main arteries for traveling about their ranges. Not only does the cover found along creeks and rivers provide the deer with safety, but much of the brush commonly found along waterways also serves as a primary browse-type food source.

Swamps, lakes and ponds, though also examples of drainages, serve whitetails in a slightly different way. As many deer hunters know, swamps are notorious for holding some of the biggest bucks in any area, simply because of the type of cover they provide. Interestingly, this kind of cover often is found around the edges of lakes and ponds. But regardless of the ac-

*Drainages always are good places to check for signs of deer activity. And it doesn't matter if the drainage is a river, creek, lake, pond or swamp.*

*Fence crossings found along field edges are good places to check for signs of buck activity. Normally, white-tailed bucks will make rubs and/or scrapes somewhere near these crossings.*

tual type of drainage, you can rest assured the whitetails in a specific area will be relating in some way to that drainage.

These are perfect places to start searching for signs of deer activity. (I do the majority of my speed-scouting in conjunction with some kind of drainage.) Walking the edges of swamps and the edges of the cover found around lakes or ponds can show you where bucks are exiting and entering those pieces of cover. And simply by following the meandering courses of rivers and creeks, you're bound to discover some well-established travel routes.

# Speed-scouting feeding areas

My second favorite place for speed-scouting is in and around feeding areas. I walk the edges of these food sources and attempt to locate which runways are playing host to the most buck traffic. In agricultural areas, I pay very close attention to any spot where the deer might have to cross a fence to enter and exit a field. White-tailed bucks seem to know that such crossing points concentrate antlerless deer activity.

Consequently, the bucks are prone to mark those spots both in a visual way (rubs) and an odorous way (scrapes). This evidence helps me determine not only if some antlered animals are visiting the field, but also the quality of those deer.

Another way, besides maps and feeding areas, to locate spots that might bear scouting is driving around during the early morning and late afternoon hours to spot deer. All this tactic requires is a little time and a good set of binoculars. I consider visual sightings of antlered animals to be the best way of confirming that a suspected area truly is worth additional effort.

In an area I'm currently hunting, I'm able to employ yet another method for pinpointing potential hot spots. The majority of the roads in that part of the state are sand-based. Because of this, I can keep informed of what's going on in certain spots merely by periodically checking for deer tracks on the roads.

A friend of mine has used this tactic almost exclusively for years. When he gets off his stand in the morning, he jumps in his pickup and slowly cruises the sandy roads that snake through the wilderness region he hunts. If he discovers a stretch of road is suddenly criss-crossed with fresh tracks, he parks his truck and heads into the woods for a quick, speed-scouting foray.

*Driving around to spot deer during the first and last hours of daylight is an excellent way to locate bucks. You then can apply a bit of speed-scouting in the immediate area.*

This guy actually spends less time scouting than most hunters I know. Yet, every year he gets several chances at huge white-tailed bucks. (Unfortunately, his shooting proficiency leaves something to be desired.) All because he has perfected his speed-scouting techniques.

As has often been mentioned, rural mail carriers, milk haulers and school bus drivers are good people to check with when attempting to locate areas that are playing host to some deer activity. And in big forest areas, you might try talking to county foresters, loggers and trappers.

# The fine points of speed-scouting

Now that you know how to decide where you should concentrate your efforts, the next step is to learn the proper behavior to adopt when speed-scouting. Believe me, knowing how to act while using this tactic may be the most important aspect of all.

When speed-scouting, I wait until the midday hours and then walk through the selected area at a rather brisk clip. I travel in high gear for two important reasons. First, I've got only limited time to accomplish my goal, so I want to cover as much ground as possible. Second, it seems that white-tailed deer don't view such behavior as threatening.

On numerous occasions I've seen deer simply stand and watch me walk right on by. Prey animals such as deer recognize predatory behavior by its posturing and/or attitude. This means that if you display a sneaky, skulking attitude when walking in the woods, any prey animal you encounter will regard you as a serious threat to its well-being. That's why it's best to keep a leisurely, "walk-through-the-woods" attitude when speed-scouting.

Besides looking for deer, I also keep my eyes peeled for any sign of buck activity, such as fresh rubs and scrapes. Once I discover such sign, I quickly walk around in the immediate area to see if there is a definite "line" of either rubs or scrapes. If so, then I follow this line until I find a suitable spot for a stand site. If the rubs and scrapes I find don't appear to be on any sort of line, then I concentrate on locating clusters of rubs or groups of scrapes. Such evidence is a good indication that a buck or bucks are visiting that particular spot on a fairly regular basis.

# Jumping bucks

If buck sign is relatively non-existent in an area, but I suspect a buck is hiding somewhere in the vicinity, then my intention is to walk until I jump that deer. My speed-scouting missions often are implemented for that very reason. I intend from the start to jump a certain buck.

This approach enables me to determine two different things. First of all, if I jump a buck during the midday hours, then it's fairly safe to assume I've discovered the location of his bedding area. Second, jumping the buck may provide me with a good enough look to ascertain if he is, indeed, a shooter. Remember, this second bit of information is important only to hunters who limit their pursuits to a certain class of bucks.

Believe it or not, I've purposely walked right through buck bedding areas during the open season. And on many occasions, I've actually jumped bucks out of those bedding areas. I realize that such behavior is viewed as strictly taboo by many "experts" in this sport. However, recent experiences have taught me otherwise.

As I stated earlier, if you look and act like a predator, a big buck definitely will view you as a threat to his well-being. Admittedly, this may prompt him to change his habits and travel patterns. However, if you display no predatory behavior, there's a good chance he'll view your intrusion as merely a temporary inconvenience. On several instances a buck I've jumped has returned a short time later to bed down in the same spot as before. Remember, all this depends upon how you act!

# Fine-tuning your stand sites

One of the major benefits of speed-scouting during the open season is that it can constantly provide you with fresh stand sites. However, it's important to give any area in which you've done some speed-scouting several days to "cool off" before actually hunting that area.

Another important thing to remember about speed-scouting: Because you have only a limited amount of time, there's a good chance your stands may prove to be just slightly out of position. But don't fret if you discover this to be the case.

If you happen to see a buck that passes by out of range, pay close attention to exactly where he walks. Then use this infor-

*Walking through buck bedding areas isn't necessarily the big "no-no" it's been made out to be. It all depends on the type of behavior you display when walking through such spots.*

mation to relocate to a position that allows you to take advantage of what you observed. However, take great pains to keep from disrupting the daily routines of the deer in that area.

Once you have scouted a territory, try to keep from making repeated speed-scouting forays into the same area. This system keeps the deer guessing about your presence. Get into the area you've selected, do your business and then get out of there. When you do return, it should be to hunt, not to scout the area further.

# Be realistic

Above all, be realistic about the amount of ground you can cover in a short time span. For instance, don't target a huge chunk of cover and then attempt to explore every square foot of that cover in one or two hours. The purpose of your mission is to become reasonably familiar with a small area, as opposed to being only slightly familiar with a much larger one.

Even though I still stress the importance of gaining complete familiarity with the areas you'll be hunting, I've found this isn't always possible. In those cases where you're very limited on time (which seems to be the case with many hunters these days), speed-scouting can provide you with just enough of the right kind of information.

# Chapter 9

# Tree Stand Placement

Initially, I had thought about titling this chapter, "Stand Placement." But after thinking it over, I decided this could prove misleading.

When hunting for white-tailed deer, I spend most of my time perched in a tree stand. And on those rare occasions when I do hunt from the ground, I'm either sneaking and peeking, or making small pushes (deer drives). I rarely stand-hunt from the ground, so I can't be considered an expert on that subject. So, whenever I mention anything in this chapter about stands, stand sites or anything of the sort, I'm referring to tree stands.

## The importance of precise stand placement

Of the many aspects of hunting for trophy white-tailed deer,

*Being out of position by just a few yards can mean a missed opportunity and an unfilled tag. Although this is more true for bow hunters, there also are cases where stand placement can be a critical factor for gun hunters.*

precise stand placement can be one of the most critical - and also one of the most frustrating. This is especially true for hunters looking to harvest a buck with archery gear. As many bow hunters will attest, being out of position by just a few yards can mean a missed opportunity and an unfilled tag.

But even if your weapon of choice happens to be a firearm of some sort, that doesn't mean you should forget about reading this chapter. Believe it or not, I've had several experiences while gun hunting for whitetails when a good buck gave me the slip simply because my stand was slightly out of position.

For this reason, I think it imperative that both bow and gun hunters learn all they can about the intricacies of precise stand placement. After all, no deer hunter wants a whopper buck to give him the slip just because the stand wasn't in the right spot.

The biggest stand placement mistake I see deer hunters make is that of setting up along the first bit of buck sign they find. Now, I'll not argue that this approach may occasionally gain a shot at a buck. However,there will be many more occasions when those hunters discover that they're out of position.

# Exceptions to the rule

I'll agree, in some instances stand selection need not be such a fine science. Often, the natural topography of the land does much to narrow down our choices. Examples that come readily to mind are brush lines found in open country and some natural funnels.

When setting up along an open-country brush line, a hunter can misplace his stand by a couple of trees and still be offered a shot. The same could happen in a funnel area such as that created when a great expanse of open ground bumps up against a narrow tree line.

In each of the above mentioned situations, stand selection may be dictated more by comfort and/or available cover than by strategic locations. This is because if and when a white-tailed buck travels through a funnel or along a brush line, he's going to be within range of nearly every tree in the funnel or brush line.

So, despite my emphasis on precision, there are some habitat types where locating the perfect spot for your stand isn't a problem. Others that come readily to mind are open, prairie-type terrain, and the type of habitat where only a few trees are large enough for mounting a tree stand.

# The one-in-a-million perfect tree

In heavily wooded areas, however, stand selection becomes much more of a precise science. Although you occasionally may get away with having your stand slightly out of position in other locations, that will very seldom happen here. In heavily forested areas, misplacing your stand by even a few yards can be costly — for bow and gun hunters alike!

This leaves us with some very tough decisions. In some situations, there could be a million trees from which to choose. Making our job even more difficult is that there may be active runways and buck sign within range of thousands of those trees.

So, how do we go about picking the one that will afford us the best chance at a buck during legal shooting hours? Although on the surface the situation may seem hopeless, it usually isn't.

Allow me to draw up a hypothetical situation. In this situation, you have a choice between two stand sites. One is in a rather open part of the forest. The other is in an area where the underbrush is thick and nearly impenetrable. It just happens that there's an equal amount of buck sign near each spot. Also, both sites are in remote areas, so the chance of interference from other hunters is rather slim.

Initially, you might opt for the stand in the thicker cover. But after considering the amount of work required, the disturbance you'll create clearing a couple of small shooting lanes, and the time needed to prepare a decent walking trail, you'd decide against this setup.

On the other hand, the stand site in the open part of the woods is pretty much ready to go as is. If you're extremely careful, you won't cause even the slightest disturbance when putting your tree stand in place. Also, there's just as much buck sign here as in the thicker cover.

Because neither spot is realizing pressure from other hunters and because there is an equal amount of buck sign near both spots, one site is just as good as the other — right? Wrong.

# Go for cover

You've forgotten to consider one very important factor: the temperament of mature white-tailed bucks. You see, their be-

*Figuring out the perfect spot for your stand often can be frustrating. Of course, the presence of thousands of trees to choose from doesn't help matters.*

*Whenever you're selecting stand sites, keep this very important fact in mind: A big buck will rarely jeopardize its safety by walking through an open area during daylight hours.*

havior remains constant, whether they are in areas of extremely heavy or light hunting pressure.

Only in a very rare case will a trophy white-tailed buck jeopardize his safety and walk through an open area during daylight hours. And after 30 years of experience, I can attest this remains true even in those open areas found miles from the nearest road or where hunting pressure is very light.

Back in the early days of my big woods hunting career, I often made the mistake of trying to kill big deer in open areas. Of course, my reasons for this were identical to those cited in the hypothetical situation.

To begin with, there was a *lot* of buck sign in the open areas I scouted. However, what convinced me that I could kill a big buck in those open areas was the fact that no one else was hunting anywhere close to me. In fact, I had every reason to believe that some of these bucks never had been hunted. Because of this, I believed that stand selection in the big woods was going to be relatively easy.

It became very obvious after only a few stand sittings that I had made a costly mistake. Oh, I was seeing bucks alright, and some of them were tremendous animals. But most of these deer were seen just at last light, skulking through thicker brush a safe distance from where I was sitting.

This taught me a very valuable and quick lesson: *When it comes to big white-tailed bucks, don't assume anything.* Even if they live a great distance from the nearest road or have relatively few encounters with humans, mature bucks are not lax in their defense skills.

I solved my problem by quickly relocating my stands into the thicker brush where I'd seen those big bucks sneaking. Almost immediately, I saw a dramatic increase in buck movement during legal shooting hours.

Of great significance was that a great deal of this activity was now taking place within 20-30 yards of my stand. I didn't have to be Einstein to figure out the importance of placement when my weapon of choice happened to be a bow.

By keeping the above-related incident in mind, you should be able to eliminate at least some of the less desirable stand sites out there. And this is just the beginning. There are several more tricks you can use to narrow down the choices even more.

# Welcome to Deer Stands 101

It seems that big white-tailed bucks love to establish travel corridors through the thickest, most impenetrable cover they can find. But along with this, they also love to use contours of the land for access routes to move from one part of their range to another. My concentrated study of rubs and rub-lines revealed just how keen white-tailed bucks are at using the lay of the land to their advantage.

As most deer hunters know, rub-lines are found along those travel routes that white-tailed bucks feel most safe and secure using. And over the past 20 years, I've walked literally hundreds of these travel routes.

*Bucks exploit topography.* The most significant lesson I've learned from walking all those rub-lines is that white-tailed bucks establish their lines of travel to take full advantage of the topography. Anything that might hide them, break up their outline or camouflage them will be exploited to its full potential.

Knowing this can be valuable when trying to figure out which is *the* best place for my stand. For instance, experience has taught me not to waste time seeking stand sites in open forested areas in a big-woods environment.

And in more open country, it means I'll search for places where a buck can move about his range while remaining tucked inside at least a little cover. Because of this, I always check any and all drainage ditches, brushy fencerows, tree lines (windbreaks), etc., for signs of buck activity.

*When all else fails, use common sense.* When searching for stand sites the best thing to do is use your common sense. Stand back, study the terrain and then give some thought to how you'd travel through that country while trying to evade somebody who was after your hide.

*Observe wind direction.* There is yet another factor that can help you decide just where your stands should be placed: wind direction. No matter what part of the country you live in, you'll find one wind direction that's predominant during your deer season. If you don't already know which wind direction is predominant, find out. Then keep this in mind when searching for stand sites.

You need to search out and prepare a few stand sites that will allow you to take advantage of every conceivable wind direction. However, set up the majority of your stands in accordance with the wind direction that's most prevalent during the open season. This factor should help you eliminate a lot of site possibilities.

# The power of observation

There are going to be times when figuring out your best possible stand option appears to be impossible. Maybe there's an equal amount of buck sign scattered throughout several different spots. Or perhaps the deer you're hunting are frequenting a food source that covers a large area (such as a stand of oak or a huge browse area).

Admittedly, trying to find *the* perfect tree under such conditions can be a trying ordeal to say the least. Often, your best efforts can wind up being nothing more than an exercise in futility. But cheer up, there is a way of locating the right tree even under these circumstances.

In chapter 6, titled, "Mastering Small Tracts," I explained at length the importance of observation. The same can be true when seeking potentially productive stand sites in heavily wooded areas. In this environment too, observation can provide you with valuable information regarding exactly where your stand should be located.

The first thing to do is walk into the targeted area, select what you think might be the right tree and put your stand in place. Then, even though you may suspect you're still somewhat out of position, go ahead and sit on this stand. (The only prerequisite is to make sure all conditions are favorable for sitting on that stand, i.e., wind direction, time of day, etc.)

Although you'll surely take a shot at a trophy buck if he happens to walk by within range, your main objective while sitting on this stand will be to observe the area. More than anything, you'll use this stand as an observation post. So as you might have guessed, a good pair of binoculars is a must.

As you sit on the stand, pay strict attention to deer movement — especially buck movement — in the area. If everything works out, one sitting should provide you with all the information you need. However, if you don't learn everything needed, sit the stand a second time. Just keep at least a three day interval between these sittings.

# Observation success stories

I used this "observation post" method to take a fine white-tailed buck with my bow in Texas during a recent season. My good friend Jack Fleming first spotted the buck using a particular travel corridor. Jack already had killed a nice buck and was in his tree stand filming with his video camera early one morning when he saw the buck. The deer was a good 200 yards away, but Jack saw enough to convince him the deer was worth setting up on. He also saw that there was a large, multi-trunked mesquite tree well within bow range of where the buck had walked.

Jack took me back to where he had seen the buck. In no time at all, I had erected a portable tree stand in the big, old mesquite. The large 9-pointer arrived nearly an hour before dark, walking along the same route he had used earlier in the day. The Patriot-tipped arrow flew true and I had my first ever bow-killed Texas whitetail.

In another case, observation was a key to eventually pinpointing a real "honey hole." Initially, my stand had been placed in a gnarly white oak standing in the middle of a small clearing. There were several huge scrapes in the clearing and at least a dozen rubs. This appeared to be *the* spot for a stand.

I sat in the stand on a late October afternoon and watched a tremendous 10-point buck sneak through the thick cover behind me. There were a couple of other such misses with bucks over the next week and a half. Interestingly, this antlered activity also took place in that same patch of cover behind the stand.

After a slight bit of scouting, I relocated the stand to a tree that let me exploit the buck activity I'd witnessed in the thick brush. Since then, my hunting partners and I have taken five bucks from that one stand. None of these deer would have been killed had we left the stand in its original position.

# Don't reveal your position

A very important point I must stress, regarding the observation method, is not to draw any attention to your position. Don't rattle or grunt or do anything to try and bring an out-of-range buck close enough for a shot.

For a mature deer especially, any unexplained sight, sound or smell can be enough to arouse suspicion, and once he's

*Precise stand placement put me in position to harvest this fine Texas whitetail. In this case, a hunting partner had determined — through a visual sighting — the exact travel pattern of the buck.*

suspicious, he becomes even harder to kill. Therefore, it's vital you keep your presence an absolute secret. You're there to observe buck travel routes and then to relocate your stand to take advantage of these routes.

# The visibility factor

Another way I narrow down my possible stand site options is by employing what I call the "visibility factor." As mentioned earlier, I've had my best luck when placing stands in thick cover. But that doesn't mean I'm going to set up in a spot where visibility is limited to only a few yards.

I like being able to see at least a little way from my stands. This affords me extra time to get ready when a buck is heading for my position. I use this criteria as yet another way to eliminate some of the many possible sites out there.

# Off-season site selection

When is the best time to look for prime stand locations? As the majority of serious deer hunters, I prefer to do the majority of my searching during the off-season — in the postseason and spring periods.

I dedicate most of my time to finding concentrations of antler rubs and scrapes. Over the years, I've found that white-tailed bucks show a great propensity for rubbing and scraping in the same places year after year. This means that if I use this information as a basis for selecting stand sites in the spring, I should be in the perfect position during the next open season.

Because of the many options available, choosing the best spot for a stand will continue to be one of the most challenging aspects of hunting for trophy deer. And, because of the unpredictable nature of mature white-tailed bucks, it also will continue to be one of the most frustrating.

Even after 30 years of chasing whitetails, deciding on *the* place for my stand continues to be something of a guessing game for me. During those 30 years, I've sat thousands of stands in hundreds of different locations and situations. To date, there have been far more unproductive than productive hours. But that is, and always will be, an undeniable reality of the sport.

# Chapter 10

# Funneling a Buck

As you probably noticed in a previous chapter, the pre-rut period is my favorite time to hunt for trophy whitetails. I've also made it quite obvious that the big woods is my favorite environment in which to hunt those animals. It only stands to reason, then, that I also have favorite spots where I prefer to place my stands in hope of taking trophy class whitetails.

During my years as a deer hunter, I've had the privilege of hunting for whitetails in a very diverse variety of geographic locations. My pursuit of these magnificent animals has led me from the cold forests of northern Canada to the hot, steamy swamps of southern Alabama. Along the way, I've also hunted almost every type of habitat in between.

## All whitetails use funnels

I've learned some very important lessons from my deer hunts in different parts of North America. First, I've learned that ma-

*After hunting whitetails from northern Canada to southern Alabama — and many points in between — I've found at least one factor remains constant. Whitetails everywhere tend to establish travel routes through existing funnels.*

ture white-tailed bucks are extremely tough customers, no matter where they're found. And second, I've found that no matter where I've hunted, the whitetails in each locale tend to establish travel routes through any sort of existing funnel.

Actually, I've heard deer hunters refer to funnels by several different names. But whether they are called bottlenecks, choke points, narrows or funnels, one thing remains constant. They are one of the best places to wait in ambush for a white-tailed buck.

The questions that are sure to follow a statement like that will include, "What exactly is a funnel?" and, "How do I go about finding one in the area I hunt?" The answers will vary a bit, according to the terrain or habitat you're hunting.

# How to identify a funnel

In the simplest terms, a funnel is any sort of narrow corridor that's found along the travel route of a white-tailed deer. To visualize this, imagine an hourglass shape. Then assume the hourglass represents the entire range covered by a white-tailed buck during his travels.

Now, if you had to choose the one place where you'd have the best chance of harvesting that buck, where would it be? More than likely, you'll answer that it's where the glass is the most narrow — the middle. This narrow section is a funnel.

A word of clarification is in order here. Although the hourglass illustration provided a perfect example of a funnel, I'm afraid there are darned few funnels you'll find while hunting that have the classic hourglass shape. Sorry.

However, that doesn't change anything about the way whitetails relate to funnels. No matter where you find whitetails, and no matter how they traverse their home ranges, those deer eventually will walk through some narrow corridor. That corridor is the funnel you are seeking.

The good news, of course, is that any time a whitetail walks through such a place, it is extremely susceptible to ambush by a predator. Deer hunters just happen to be a deer's number one predator.

All kinds of natural occurrences may force whitetails to travel through these narrow corridors. Water, whether in the form of a river, creek, lake or beaver pond, may cause funneling. And in more "developed" areas, man-made objects such as

*No matter where you find whitetails, or how they traverse their home ranges, eventually those deer will walk through a narrow corridor. This corridor, whether natural or man-made, is a funnel.*

buildings, roads, fence lines and open ground may force whitetails to funnel through certain spots.

Changes in elevation also may prompt whitetails to establish travel routes through certain locations. It may be an extremely high ridge that they'd rather walk around than over. Or it might be a swamp they prefer to skirt instead of slog through.

Regardless of what it might be, when an existing situation dictates walking through a certain spot, whitetails are restricted to a rather narrow travel corridor. And somewhere in this narrow corridor — or funnel — is where your stand should be placed.

As mentioned before, I've seen perfect examples of funnels in every type of white-tailed deer habitat I've hunted. Following is a breakdown of each of those habitats and, more importantly, where you can expect to find funnels.

# Funnels in open country

Let's face it, trophy class white-tailed bucks display a great aversion for venturing into any open area. This is true even when those deer are under the influence of peak rut. Because of this aversion, our job of finding funnels in open country is easier than in other kinds of terrain.

Brushy fence lines, for example, are an excellent example of where you might find preferred buck travel routes. Most times, these brushy fence lines link one patch of cover to another. Hence, they are bound to serve as main arteries for traveling whitetails.

By sticking close to brush lines, whitetails are afforded at least a small amount of cover when traveling across vast stretches of otherwise treeless terrain. Let the presence of rubs and scrapes indicate exactly which fence lines are harboring the most antlered activity.

As is often the case in open, prairie-type habitat common in some Western and Midwestern states, waterways provide the only adequate deer cover. So saying then, river and creek bottoms are another place where you'll no doubt find some concentrated whitetail activity. However, merely establishing a stand site anywhere along either of these drainages is not a sure ticket to success.

Granted, most of the available cover is found only along rivers or creeks, but I've seen examples where that cover is quite expansive — sometimes more than a mile in width. In such

*Bushy fence lines often connect one piece of cover with another.
It therefore stands to reason that they will most likely serve as
the main arteries for any and all bucks in the area.*

situations, a buck has plenty of cover in which to continually evade you. Obviously then, your job is to find a place where that expanse of cover funnels into a more narrow corridor. And the best place to look for a funnel in river or creek bottom country is where an expanse of open country pushes up almost to the banks of the waterway. (Often, sharp bends or turns in the waterway will create such a condition.)

When this happens, usually the brush or timber found along the edge of the waterway will be squeezed down to a thin strip. Because undisturbed whitetails aren't crazy about walking either in the water or the open field, they're left with walking through the thin sliver of cover as they travel along the water.

In most instances where I've seen the above-mentioned situation, I've discovered a single, well-worn runway just inside the edge of cover. The deer in the area had been funneled down to using a single travel route in order to use the narrow strip of cover. All that remained for me at that point was finding a tree suitable for my stand.

# Funnels in hill and bluff country

Deer hunters who dedicate their efforts to hill and/or bluff country whitetails may find funnels in several different locations. In my experience, the most common, productive and easiest of all funnels to find in this terrain are saddles or swales along hilltops.

I've learned whitetails are basically lazy creatures — especially older age-class bucks. In fact, much as humans do, they prefer to travel about their ranges via a route that provides them with the easiest going.

Going up and over a hill or bluff at its highest point makes no more sense for the deer then it does for you or me. Exploiting the terrain to its fullest, therefore, means finding a way to ascend, cross over and reach the other side of hills or bluffs with the least expenditure of energy. In that regard, saddles are the most likely and certainly the most natural way of accomplishing this task.

Locating saddles in hill country is a relatively easy chore. Just stand back and survey the overall lay of the land in your hunting area. Notice the very tops of the hills, then let your eyes casually follow the contour of these hilltops.

Occasionally, you'll notice a stretch of the hilltop that's slightly lower than the surrounding terrain. This is what I've come to call a saddle. A closer investigation likely will show that at least one well-traveled runway goes through the middle of that saddle. Once more, all that's left is to locate a stand site that lets you take advantage of this funnel.

# Funnels in big woods

When I began hunting in the big woods of my home state, Wisconsin, my biggest concern was locating areas of concentrated buck activity. Initially, it appeared as though I might have better luck attempting to find a contact lens in a haystack. My first outings in this environment left me thinking that the deer herd was very nomadic, given to wandering aimlessly through all parts of its range.

However, a bit more study on the subject showed me that there definitely were special, predictable spots where big woods deer walked whenever they traveled through a certain area. As you might imagine, this nugget of information really grabbed my attention.

I soon realized that the most common and easily located natural funnels in any big woods terrain are those fingers of high ground that run through an area of low, swampy ground. Even though the change in elevation may be slight (often, these funnels don't show up on a topographical map), they'll still be used as a main travel corridor by the deer.

Similarly, strips of high ground that run between lakes, potholes or even beaver ponds also can be bottlenecks of deer activity in big woods. I've lost count of the many bucks that I've taken in one or the other of the above described funnel types.

One such funnel stand of mine has consistently produced big woods bucks, not only for me, but for two of my brothers as well. Over a ten-year period, each of us has managed to take an almost equal number of bucks from that one funnel area.

As with any type of funnel, these fingers of high ground can vary substantially in size. The best of these funnels to hunt are those only a few yards wide with a single runway coursing down the middle. (This is as close as you'll get to the classic hourglass design.)

On the other hand, I've found and hunted fingers of high ground that were at least 100 yards wide and had several different runways snaking through them. Of course, it's obvious which funnel type is more conducive to a high success rate, because a wide finger gives the deer more chances to evade me.

I look at it this way. Trying to harvest a trophy buck while giving him several different ways to evade me is similar to my playing golf with a PGA pro. More times than not, I'll lose. Conversely, if I hunt a funnel with only *one* active runway through it and a buck passes through that funnel while I'm set up there, the odds are in my favor.

Another funnel type found in big woods exists where a gradually narrowing point of high ground protrudes into surrounding low ground or thicker cover. I've observed that this point of high ground becomes the main vein of travel for every deer passing through that particular spot.

When returning to the swamp or thick cover in the morning, a deer will walk down the entire length of the point, browsing and checking out its surroundings as it goes. It will slip into the low ground or thick cover (which probably serves as a bedding area) right off the tip of the point.

In the evening, that deer will use the same route when it exits the low ground or thick cover. Instead of exiting the swamp just anywhere, a deer usually will ascend to the higher ground at the very end of the point.

The very tip of the point, because of its narrowing feature, is going to funnel the movements of the deer into a relatively small area. Where to position your stand advantageously should be quite obvious.

## Funnels and man-made obstacles

One of the best bow hunting stand sites I've had was created by the introduction of cattle into a woodlot I'd been hunting. The day those cattle were turned loose, the resident deer herd abandoned that part of the woods being pastured.

The deer avoided the cattle by following the outside of the fence that bordered the pasture on one side. In only a couple outings I discovered this new travel corridor and quickly realized I was looking at a man-made funnel. In a few minutes I had my tree stand in place.

On a cold, late-October morning a week later, five different bucks walked by within bow range. And on subsequent hunts deer activity I saw convinced me that the newly erected fence and introduction of cattle were the best thing that could have happened to me.

Houses, barns, sheds or buildings of any kind are other man-made obstacles that can have a great funneling effect on white-tailed deer. In fact, I recently talked with a highly successful bow hunter who has used "urban sprawl" to his benefit.

"The terrain in the area I hunt," he told me, "is made up of small patches of woods with a lot of open ground in between. The problem had always been that there were just too many of these small patches. You never knew which one the deer were going to use on any given day.

"However, this all changed when people starting building houses in a lot of those small patches of woods. Of course, the influx of people eliminated a lot of the woods the deer could use for cover and travel. Because of this, they've been forced to funnel the majority of their activity into just a few patches of woods."

Once this hunter had found exactly which woodlots were hosting the majority of deer activity, his success rate soared. At last count, he had arrowed five bucks that qualified for entry into the Pope & Young record book.

In most cases, funnels are located along routes used by deer in their normal, undisturbed travel patterns. These funnels thus can be hotspots anytime during the season. Still, there's one period of time that I've found to be far better than any other for hunting these covert corridors. The pre-rut period.

# Funnels and the pre-rut period

As my chapter on hunting the pre-rut vividly points out, white-tailed bucks become highly active at this time of year. But unlike the breeding period, when there seems to be no rhyme or reason for their behavior, white-tailed bucks in the pre-rut are fairly predictable and, if such a thing is possible, somewhat patternable.

In every habitat I've hunted, I've seen that bucks love to establish rub-lines leading into funnels. In addition, they'll also open several scrapes right in the heart of a funnel.

I've concluded that white-tailed bucks know funnels concentrate the activities of all the deer in specific area. They seem aware that a funnel serves as a hub for buck-doe and buck-buck interaction.

*White-tailed bucks love to establish rub-lines leading into funnels. This knowledge has led me to some of my finest trophies.*

I've used this bit of knowledge frequently to my advantage. Calling, both rattling and grunting, has been extremely effective when used in conjunction with a funnel stand.

# Deer are suspicious in funnels

Hunting these spots, however, requires extreme care. In all my years of hunting, I've yet to see a mature whitetail approach and then walk through a funnel without displaying utmost concern for its own safety. It seems as though a white-tailed deer realizes that passing through a funnel puts it at great risk from any of its natural predators. Therefore, before heading into the narrow corridor, it spends a bit of time checking for the presence of any threats.

Because whitetails display this behavior near funnels, you must give a great deal of thought to setting up in these areas. First, establish walking routes that get you into and out of the spot without alerting the deer. Second, use every conceivable piece of natural cover to prevent your being spotted while on the stand. And lastly, never occupy any funnel stand if you suspect wind direction might compromise your position.

No technique for hunting white-tailed deer, no matter how refined or perfected, can guarantee success every time out. I believe most deer hunters are fully aware of and accept this fact. (If hunting were ever to suddenly become easy or routine, the allure of this sport would be lost.)

Still, there are tactics that can prove consistently effective. Funnel hunting is one such tactic. Although it won't guarantee success, I believe that becoming proficient at locating and setting up in funnels can increase the success rate of any deer hunter — no matter what sort of terrain that hunter uses.

*Whitetails seem aware that traveling through funnels puts them at risk of attack by predators. For that reason, they usually display a heightened caution near these areas.*

# Chapter 11

# B.O. Is Bad News

Okay, it's an offensive, in-your-face title. But, somehow, "Making Sense Of The Scent Issue" didn't really seem any more appropriate. Whatever the case, this chapter is going to deal with the intricacies of adopting an aggressive approach to the human odor problem.

I'll readily agree that this subject has received a great deal of attention in recent years, but there's good reason for all this attention. Even after all that's been written and said on the subject, many deer hunters apparently still haven't caught the importance of going odor-free. I'm convinced that one of the biggest reasons so many hunters end their seasons with unfilled tags is because they ignored the principles of odor control.

Throughout this chapter I'll frequently refer to "human odor." However, don't get the impression that I'm talking only about odors associated with the human body. When I mention human odor, I mean any odor that white-tailed deer might as-

*In my opinion, the biggest reason many hunters end their seasons with unfilled tags is that those hunters have failed to grasp the importance of odor control.*

sociate with humans. And when I use the term "odor-free," I mean free of all *human* odor.

At the top of this list is personal body odor, caused mostly by perspiration and (although not mentioned very often) an unclean crotch area. Other odors whitetails readily associate with humans include petroleum products, colognes and after shaves, and cooking odors. There are, of course, many others as well, but those listed here are the main culprits.

# The importance of going odor-free

I'm continually astounded by the number of hunters who query me each year about the importance of going odor-free. Two of the most often asked questions are, "Do you really take a shower before each time you go out in the woods?" and "Do you really think going odor-free is worth all the extra effort?" The answer to those two questions is a profound, *yes!*

There's good reason for my aggressive approach to the human odor problem: In the years since I've cleaned up my act, my success rate on mature bucks has increased tremendously. And I know that mine is not an isolated case. Every one of the more serious and successful trophy whitetail hunters I know has incorporated the same odorless approach into his hunting efforts.

I think the reason many deer hunters refuse to show any concern about human odor is because those hunters are convinced there's nothing they can do about human odor. As one hunter told me recently, "It's impossible to totally eliminate human odor anyway. So why should I even try?"

I agree it is impossible to *totally* eliminate human odor. However, I've seen incidents in which my human odors were sufficiently weakened or camouflaged to temporarily fool a big buck's nose. This alone has given me the edge I've needed to harvest more than just a couple of mature bucks.

# Simple secrets of eliminating odor

The first step toward achieving an odor-free state is washing all your hunting clothes, including underwear, in one of the odorless hunting detergents now on the market. As soon as the wash cycle is finished, remove the clothes from the washer and hang them outside to line dry.

*While it is impossible to fully erase human odor, I do believe you can weaken and/or camouflage your odor enough to fool a big buck's nose temporarily. This fact has given me the edge needed to take a number of trophies.*

I wash my clothes several weeks in advance of the season. I then leave them on the line for up to a week, hoping for a good rain to cleanse them even further. Once they have dried completely, I remove the clothes from the line and seal them in plastic garbage bags.

Some hunters take leaves, plants or even foods native to the areas they're hunting and enclose these in the bags with their clothing. They do this so their clothing will absorb the odors of these items. I see nothing wrong with this, and have done it myself on a couple occasions. It really does seem to help.

Even on extremely cold weather hunts, I keep those clothes sealed in the plastic bags until I reach my hunting area. Once at the area, I then change into my hunting duds. If the weather is warm, or if I'll have a long walk to my stand site, I'll carry the heavier clothes in a daypack, waiting until I reach my stand before donning this last layer.

Of course, ensuring that your hunting clothes are odor-free is absolutely pointless if you don't take time to deodorize your body. Here's my routine. Just before going out to hunt, I shower, washing my entire body with a bacteria-killing, odorless soap. (I shower before each and every hunt, which frequently is twice a day.)

Once out of the shower, I dry off with a towel that's been washed in odorless detergent. I then apply odorless, bacteria-killing deodorant to my underarms. The kind I use was specifically formulated with deer hunters in mind.

Next, I dress in clothes (not my hunting clothes) that also have been washed in odorless detergent — so my body won't acquire new smells. Then I immediately head out the door to my truck and drive to the hunting area.

I try to avoid making any stops along the way — especially to do something such as put gas in my vehicle. In fact, once I'm showered and odor-free, I tend to stay away from all gas stations and convenience stores.

Once at my hunting site, I change into my hunting clothes. When the hunt is over, I change out of my hunting clothes and into the clothes I wore previously. My hunting clothes go back into the plastic garbage bag.

I frequently check my clothing to see if it might be getting "smelly." And if I suspect a piece of my clothing may have become contaminated with a human odor, my entire outfit goes back for the washing and drying routine. (As a safety measure, I keep an extra set of odor-free camouflaged clothing stored in a plastic bag and ready to go.)

Whitetails also can sniff out human presence because of footwear. In most cases, I avoid wearing all-leather boots, because leather absorbs and holds foreign odors for long periods of time. If I wear "contaminated" leather boots into my hunting areas, these odors will be transferred to the ground with every step I take.

I wear pac-type boots on just about all my hunts. These rubber-bottomed, leather-topped boots are now manufactured in a variety of weights, which means I can find a pair designed for almost any temperature range.

# What about scents and scent killers?

Several years ago, I began carrying a bottle of B-Scent-Free odor-killing spray with me on all my hunts. If I'm perspiring when I reach the stand, I spray a mist over my head, the inside of my hat, my crotch area and the tops of my boots. Usually, the mist dries off within minutes.

Do these odor-killing sprays really work? I've witnessed a couple of incidents on a bow hunt in Alberta, Canada, where coyotes were unable to sniff out my tracks after I had applied the spray to my boots. Interestingly, on days when I hadn't used the spray, the coyotes could smell my tracks from several feet away. Yes, this stuff does work!

# Deer urine: the smell of success

Until four years, I shunned any type of cover scent when hunting for trophy whitetails, simply because I hadn't found any cover scent that didn't alarm deer. I had tried coyote, bobcat, fox and even skunk scents. And I'd seen instances in which each of these scents had put whitetails instantly on alert.

In my opinion, nothing could be more reassuring or instill confidence in deer like the smell of other deer. So for years I had insisted that if someone wanted to devise an effective cover scent for whitetails, they should bottle pure deer urine.

During the late 1980s, Larry Harris of Bruce, Wisconsin, decided to do just that. He gave me a bottle of the urine scent to try a few years ago and the results were nothing short of phenomenal.

144

*Predator type cover scents, such as skunk, fox, bobcat and coyote, actually are an alarming odor for whitetails. Nothing can reassure and instill confidence in deer like the smell of urine from other deer.*

*Whitetails often are able to detect human presence long after a hunter has left the woods — merely because of poor footwear selection. If at all possible, wear synthetic-soled boots and avoid leather.*

Bucks, does and fawns all seem enamored by the urine-based scent. What I really like, however, is that the scent does double duty as both a cover and an attractant. Also, I'm very impressed that, to this day, I've not seen one deer go on the alert after smelling the scent. In fact, the scent seems to have a calming, confidence-instilling effect on whitetails.

It's very important to remember that using cover scents and odor-killing sprays never is an excuse to hunt a stand when the wind is blowing from a compromising direction. Also, the use of such products, no matter how good you may think they are, is not an excuse to forego keeping both your body and clothing in an odor-free state.

## Where there's smoke...

About ten years ago, I stumbled onto another cover scent that I've taken to using whenever I hunt a certain area in my home state. Since the day I first learned of this effective and natural cover scent, I've talked to many trophy hunters who also employ the same technique. Let me explain.

When staying at my cabin in northern Wisconsin, I often hang my hunting clothes on a line strung between two trees. I burn wood at my cabin, and one day, the wind happened to blow the wood smoke right toward my clothesline. Later, when I retrieved the clothes from the line, I found they were permeated with wood-smoke odor.

Having no extra hunting clothes with me that day, I had no choice but to wear the smoke-drenched clothing. That afternoon, several deer crossed my walking trail near my stand. And to my amazement, a mature doe walked directly behind me, crossing right through my scent-stream. None of those big-woods deer displayed the slightest reaction to the wood-smoke odor.

Later, I pondered over the incident. Just about everybody living in that part of the state had a wood-burning furnace in their home. This meant that, from the time the first cold weather hit in the fall until the warming days of spring arrived, the smell of wood smoke was everywhere. From all indications, it seemed the deer had gotten used to this smell.

# Keep rotating

Throughout this book, I've stressed the importance of continually rotating your stand sites. The B.O. problem is yet another good reason to adopt this policy into your hunting efforts.

The more trips you make into a certain spot, especially on consecutive days, the greater the likelihood that spot will become contaminated with human odor. And there's a possibility of this happening even if you take an aggressive approach to controlling human odor.


# Stories for the skeptical

So maybe you're one of those who thinks being careful about human odor when deer hunting is a bunch of baloney. Or maybe you're one of those who thinks that I'm overrating the whitetails' sense of smell. If you fit into one of those categories, consider the following two stories.

I've related the following story in articles for a couple of national magazines. I've done so because it so vividly points out the amazing ability of white-tailed deer to detect suspicious odors. Therefore, I think it bears repeating. (This incident occurred in the late-1970s, before I became an odor-free deer hunter.)

In the week prior to opening day of archery season, I had been watching three deer come out each evening to feed in an alfalfa field. To this point, the deer had been undisturbed, so I could just about set my watch by their appearance.

Slightly after 6:00 p.m., a big doe would walk into the field, followed a minute later by her fawn from that year. Five minutes after these two deer appeared, a sleek eight-point buck would edge into the field. The routine was exactly the same every evening.

On opening day I waited until 9:30 a.m. before heading to the alfalfa field and putting up my stand. At the last moment, one of my hunting partners decided to accompany me on the stand-placement mission. Not knowing any better, I consented.

I soon found the perfect tree for my portable stand. The big pine was situated just 15 yards from the runway I had seen the deer use to enter the field. Immediately, I went to work situating my stand in the tree. While putting the finishing touches on my stand site, I noticed that my partner no longer was standing silently below the tree. I quickly looked around and saw him walking through the woods — on the runway the deer used every evening.

With a soft whistle, I got his attention and motioned him back. By the time he reached me, I had descended to the ground. We hurriedly gathered up my gear and headed for the road.

I was on the stand that very afternoon. Shortly after 6:00 p.m., the doe walked into view, the fawn trailing a few yards behind. From her actions, it was apparent the deer were unaware that anything might be different. But that suddenly changed when the doe reached the spot where my buddy had walked earlier in the day. (By the way, he had worn leather boots.)

Immediately, her whole demeanor changed. Instead of being relaxed and unconcerned, she now was nervous and alert. The doe first smelled and then started following my buddy's tracks. It took her only moments to decide something was wrong. At that point, she and her youngster turned and walked into some nearby thick cover. I never saw the doe, her fawn or the eight-pointer feeding in the alfalfa field again that fall.

Here was a case of a white-tailed deer picking up the scent of and accurately tracking a man whose trail had been made eight hours earlier. To this day I remain impressed by this feat. However, I recently learned of an even more amazing event.

While talking to a fellow deer hunter, he casually asked me if I had any idea how long human odor remains in the woods. I answered that it would depend on how concentrated that bit of odor was, but that I always had understood most human odor would fully dissipate in 24 hours. Upon hearing this, the man related a story about something he had seen the previous season.

It seems he'd been trimming a shooting lane near one of his stand sites and happened to grab a bush with his bare hand. At the time, he gave little thought to the incident. The man waited until the afternoon of the following day before returning to sit on his stand.

"I was there for about an hour before the first deer, a doe, showed up," he stated. "She was walking along, browsing and totally relaxed, and then she came alongside that bush I had grabbed the day before."

*Whitetail bucks are much more keen than antlerless deer at detecting human odor. It's a fact that they react to much smaller amounts of such odor.*

He watched the doe as she spent several minutes smelling the bush. Then she snapped her head erect, looked around and started stamping a front foot. After about 30 seconds of stamping, she snorted, wheeled and ran into a nearby patch of thick cover. Even though more than 24 hours had passed since the hunter had grasped the bush, the doe had sensed some human odor.

These are two perfect illustrations of the highly refined sense of smell possessed by white-tailed deer. Even more interesting is that both the above incidents involved antlerless deer.

In my opinion, mature white-tailed bucks are even more keen on detecting human odor — and they react to smaller amounts of such odor. So it only stands to reason that you should use extra caution when dealing with these animals.

# The reality behind dumb luck

As illustrated previously, cleaning up your act and adopting an odorless approach for your hunting ventures really doesn't entail much extra effort. However, the little bit of effort you invest can pay off in a big way.

Of course, I've run into people who contest every word written about the precautions needed when pursuing mature whitetails. Usually, these are people who have killed a tremendous buck, but did so without adhering to *any* of the basic guidelines for hunting trophy whitetails. Such was the case of a hunter I ran into a few years back.

This individual had shot a huge 12-point buck during our gun deer season. "I was sitting on a big ol' stump, smoking a cigarette when the buck showed up," the hunter told me. "I let him walk within 30 yards before I pulled the trigger. Guess that just proves all this stuff about human odor and scent is a bunch of baloney!"

When I questioned the man as to whether the buck had approached from the upwind or downwind side, he just looked at me. "How the heck am I supposed to know," he answered. "I don't pay any attention to that kind of stuff."

It's obvious that the 12-pointer had come in from the upwind side of the hunter. It's also apparent the "big ol' stump" on which he was sitting must have provided the hunter with adequate camouflage.

Unfortunately, guys like this hunter think that killing a single big buck makes them an expert on every facet of deer hunting. To them, it makes no difference that their accomplishment was a direct result of nothing more than pure dumb luck.

I'm a firm believer that luck plays at least some role in all successful hunts. I also believe, however, that you can increase your luck tremendously by taking an aggressive approach to *all* aspects of this sport. This is especially true when dealing with bucks and B.O.

# Chapter 12

# Small Drives = Big Results

As most serious trophy whitetail hunters, I've always preferred going up against my quarry one-on-one. This, in my opinion, is the most effective approach for dealing with the extremely sensitive and reclusive nature of mature bucks.

I greatly enjoy applying my expertise and hunting abilities, and trusting my own judgment when attempting to "figure out" a big buck. Believe me, harvesting a trophy animal after doing everything myself is a truly rewarding experience. Therein lies much of the attraction of this sport.

## When solo hunting doesn't work

When gun hunting for whitetails, however, there are instances in which stand hunting, sneaking and peeking, or any other type of solo methods just aren't productive. In such instances I employ a technique that requires dependence on the abilities and expertise of several other hunters. This is the technique of small drives for big bucks.

As a matter of clarification, the term "small drives" does not refer to driving whitetails on small tracts of land. Rather, "small" describes the number of hunters involved — two being the minimum and five the maximum.

My hunting partners and I have seen small drives produce well both on small tracts of land and also in big woods regions. We've seen the method produce enough times to know it's not an accident when we score on a monster buck.

# Why gang drives don't work

Before getting into the nuts and bolts of making effective small drives for big bucks, I'd like to explain why I think traditional gang driving is an ineffective method for taking mature whitetail bucks. I came to the realization many years ago that gang driving whitetails held absolutely no appeal for me. There were a couple of reasons for this.

First, I've never been a big fan of hunting with large groups of hunters. Second, I quickly concluded that gang driving is one of the least productive tactics for taking trophy whitetails consistently.

Common sense shows why the majority of deer taken on gang drives usually are antlerless animals and immature bucks. Simply put, long before the drive ever begins, the mature bucks in the targeted area figure out what's going on. They then take the necessary steps to evade both drivers and standers. My brief experiences with gang driving for whitetails taught me that the greater the number of hunters employed, the greater the chance that somebody will do something to alert the deer in the drive area. These errors usually are committed *before* the drive ever starts.

These hunter blunders are the reason big bucks in the drive area catch on to the game plan. And once they know what's happening, they'll figure out an effective escape strategy — long before that game plan is executed.

If you ever have been, or might still be, involved in gang driving whitetails, you'll have to admit, it's darned hard to keep secret a large group of hunters. The slamming of a car door, a shout, a cough, the chambering of a shell, or a noisy entrance into the woods are all tip-offs to big bucks in the area that something's up.

Once alerted, these animals have two choices. They can quickly vacate the vicinity or burrow even deeper into some impenetrable thicket, refusing to move unless a hunter nearly steps on them. (And even if they are jumped, chances are they'll run out the back of the drive.)

In either case, the results usually are the same. The only deer seen by the standers will be antlerless animals and immature bucks. Only in very rare cases will large gang drives manage to run a true, trophy class buck past a waiting gun.

Once a wise old buck suspects he's being forced toward a certain direction, he'll refuse to go that way. If this means lying tight and allowing a driver to walk past almost within spitting distance, he'll do it. (I've witnessed big bucks pulling this stunt.)

Another effective escape tactic I've seen big bucks use is completely vacating an area at the first hint of danger. In most cases when this occurs, the bucks hear a suspicious noise and clear out long before the standers have reached their positions.

## Why small drives gain big bucks

The main reason our small drives are so effective is that we take great pains to keep the deer from suspecting that they are being driven. Another factor that helps us greatly is the way we make our drives. If at all possible, we refrain from making a drive in exactly the same manner twice in a row.

Gang drivers are notorious for repeating their drives, in exactly the same manner, day after day. With this approach, even the does and fawns in that area catch on to exactly where the drivers are going to walk, where the standers will be waiting, and how much time is available to flee. They then adjust their escape strategies accordingly.

Another reason our small drives are so successful is that all of us making these drives are extremely familiar with the areas being hunted. This knowledge of the country and how it lays is critical for establishing exactly where the drivers should walk to jump bedded deer and where the standers should set up.

*Wait until midmorning before making small drives, thus ensuring that the bucks are back in their bedding areas. This is exactly where you want them.*

# How to set up a successful small drive

Our basic plan of attack finds us waiting until midmorning before making our first drive of the day. Starting at this time of day ensures that most bucks will have long since retired to their bedding areas. And that's exactly where we want them.

First we have our one or more standers walk in and set up along known escape routes. Getting to these ambush points undetected is a key priority. If this means walking great distances to accomplish the task, we'll do it.

Once our standers are in position, our driver approaches from an upwind direction and slowly walks through any spot he suspects might be holding a buck. Contrary to gang driving behavior, our driver doesn't shout, whistle or make any unnecessary noise. Rather, he walks through the woods as if taking a stroll.

Although he doesn't shout or whistle, at no time does our driver attempt to hide his presence. He wants the bucks both to see and smell him. When this happens, the bucks become so preoccupied with the invader behind them that they pay less attention to what's in front of them. On some occasions we've taken bucks that were spending more time watching out for the hunter behind them than looking for danger ahead.

If our driver is able to determine that he has jumped a buck, he slowly tags along behind the buck. A number of such experiences have shown us that, when convinced they're dealing with only one hunter, big bucks are more apt to attempt a straight-line escape.

Above all, it's important that the driver never acts in a sneaky manner. The trick is to keep a jumped buck fully aware of exactly where the driver is at all times. If he's totally concentrating on evading this guy, there's little chance that he'll detect the standers.

As stated earlier, we use anywhere from two to five people when making our drives. However, the only time we employ an equal number of drivers and standers is when only two people are involved. At all other times we prefer to have more standers than drivers. Because we're so familiar with the areas being hunted, we don't need lots of people to get a big buck up and moving. In most cases, one person can accomplish this task.

A driver never should act in a "sneaky" manner. Make sure the driven buck is aware of exactly where the driver is at all times. If the buck is concentrating fully on the driver, there's little chance of his detecting one of the standers.

# Driving on unfamiliar land

On the other hand, choosing exactly which escape route that buck is going to use is quite another matter. That's why we prefer to have more standers than drivers. The more standers we have, the more escape routes we can cover. (We've often taken a group of five and split it into one driver and four standers.)

In the event we happen to be hunting an area we're not familiar with, then the best we can do is select "deery" looking spots to send our driver through. And when picking out stand sites in strange areas, we simply use a bit of basic woodsmanship to select sites we think might provide a shot at a fleeing buck.

Although this is nothing more than guesswork at best, it's really the only way of learning what's going on in a strange area. As reassurance, just about every piece of cover in which my hunting partners and I now make drives was strange land to us at one time. But after making only one or two pushes through those spots, we knew exactly where to walk to jump the biggest bucks.

In the same vein, our initial stand site selections often left us just slightly out of position. However, we paid attention to where we saw driven bucks running and then adjusted our stand sites to take advantage of those newly discovered escape routes. Ideally, only one close call with a big buck should reveal *exactly* where to stand next time.

# "Leapfrogging" through big woods

When making drives in big woods areas with which I'm not familiar, I like to employ a technique I've come to call "leapfrogging." This technique enables my partners and me to effectively hunt a rather expansive piece of real estate, while quickly learning the exact lay of the land.

We first select a large piece of "deery" looking cover. We then have our standers circle around and take up positions several hundred yards ahead. At an arranged time the driver walks through the spots showing the most promise.

When the driver reaches the standers, the roles are reversed. (The driver now become a stander and vice-versa.) We then continue this process until we either run out of time or woods.

An initial stand site selection, especially in a strange area, may leave you slightly out of position. If that's the case, simply pay attention to where any driven bucks run. Then use this information to your advantage the next time you "push" that same piece of cover.

*Another big woods buck that fell victim to a small drive. I shot this thick-necked 8-pointer on a "leapfrogging" type drive through a huge poplar slash.*

On some occasions we've spent nearly an entire day leapfrogging through one huge tract of land.

One leapfrogging episode several years ago resulted in my taking a big Northwoods buck. The parcel of cover we were hunting that day was a five-year-old poplar slash covering hundreds of acres. We already had leapfrogged through two, quarter-mile long pieces of the cover without incident.

On the third drive it once again was my turn to stand. I circled around and took up a position on top of a high hill. My vantage point allowed me to watch several ridges that extended out of the slash and sloped gently down to a nearby creek bottom.

Not long after the drive started, I noticed movement directly below me. I riveted my attention on the spot and quickly made out the form of a large buck slowly working his way down one of the ridges, no doubt headed for the creek bottom. One shot from my .270 put the brute eight-pointer down for keeps.

When leapfrogging, we always keep our eyes open for any sign that might indicate we're in a potentially productive area. Fresh rubs, scrapes and/or tracks are all good indicators. Of course, actually seeing antlered animals is always a tip-off that we've discovered a hot spot.

# Driving by "walking drag"

Another effective driving tactic we've recently adopted is simply called "walking drag." Although this tactic can work well with two hunters, it's ideal when three are involved.

We have one hunter slowly start making his way through a targeted area. He walks in a relatively straight line, heading into the wind. Fifteen to 20 minutes later, two more hunters start in the same area, walking roughly 100 yards to each side of the first hunter's path.

If everything goes the way it's supposed to, any buck jumped by the "point" man will circle around, catch his wind and then sneak out behind him. Eventually, one of the two hunters walking drag should get a chance at the buck.

My brother Jeff and I used this tactic effectively while hunting a large section of real estate in northern Wisconsin several years ago. On that day, I was the point man and Jeff was walking drag 20 minutes behind me.

About 45 minutes into the hunt I jumped a tremendous buck, but couldn't get a clear shot. The deer quickly circled

*This big woods 9-pointer was taken by my brother Jeff by use of the "walking-drag" method. This tactic can be extremely effective on bucks that just won't cooperate on a normal drive.*

around, caught my wind and took off in Jeff's direction. Several minutes later, I heard my brother fire one shot. The 9-pointer had beautiful, mahogany colored antlers and a dressed weight of 190 pounds.

We've found the walking drag approach is an effective way of dealing with big bucks that we just can't get to cooperate on our normal small drives. Such bucks, whenever jumped, circle around and run out the back of our drive. The walking drag catches them.

# Bucks prefer a tailwind — really

Except when employing the walking drag method, we prefer to drive big bucks in a downwind direction. That's right, I said we prefer to get the bucks going in a *downwind* direction. But before you question my sanity, let me explain something.

Setting up to push deer into the wind is a big reason so many deer drives fail. To this day, I see many groups of hunters trying to drive bucks into the wind. When I ask them why they do this, their replies go something like, "Because everybody knows a big buck will always run into the wind." Oh really?

Contrary to what you may have read or been told, big whitetail bucks don't always run into the wind. In fact, my partners and I have observed that most of the mature bucks we've jumped preferred to travel downwind. With this fact in hand, it's been easier for us to get a big buck to go where we want him to go.

My reasoning for a driven buck preferring to "tailwind it" is that, more than anything, he wants to keep track of the human behind him. And the only way he can do this, while at the same time remaining a safe distance ahead, is by using his nose. So he'll run with the wind at his tail, trusting his eyes to warn him of any dangers ahead.

The first time I saw a big buck employ the tailwinding strategy was during a gun deer season back in the early 1970s. My dad and I had spent the better part of a day pushing and tracking a big buck through some wooded bluffs near our home. The big deer kept the wind at his tail for most of the time we chased him. Because of what we had always heard about whitetails, my dad and I found it hard to believe what we were seeing. Since that day, however, I've seen big bucks display this behavior many times.

But the fact that a driven buck has sacrificed his sense of smell doesn't make him a pushover. If anything, a buck that runs with the wind on his tail seems to turn up his visual acuity a couple of notches. For this reason, standers should seek ambush points that provide not only a fairly decent field of fire, but also adequate cover.

If you remain convinced that the only way to drive deer is into the wind, then let me ask you a question. How do you expect to push a mature whitetail buck past one of your standers if that buck is going to smell the waiting hunter long before he comes into sight? I rest my case.

## Small drives really are better

Or maybe you're of the opinion that if you use enough hunters, gang driving is bound to be effective. Wrong. A large number of drivers will *not* ensure that you'll chase every single deer out of any patch of cover you attack. Let me tell you a story that supports my assertion.

I had spent the better part of the day tracking a small eight-point buck over snow-covered ground. During the course of his travels, that buck had actually walked right into and then safely out of several large, "organized" deer drives.

In one case, the eight-pointer slipped into a very small woodlot that was being driven. Granted, the underbrush was rather thick, but there had to have been at least 15 hollering and whistling hunters walking through the tiny woodlot. It didn't appear as though they could miss anything.

I stood back and held my breath, waiting to hear a barrage of shooting begin any second in the open field on the far end of the woods being driven. Unbelievably, not a single shot rang out.

Within minutes of being organized, the drive was over. The hunters regrouped, drew up a quick plan to deal with another woodlot down the road, then climbed into their vehicles and took off.

As soon as the last carload of hunters had disappeared over a distant hill, I jumped back on the eight-pointer's track. Just a short way into the woods, I found where the buck had suddenly dropped to his belly, obviously to escape detection from a couple of the drivers. (Tracks in the snow showed me two noisy hunters actually had walked within 15 yards of the buck.)

Amazingly, when the buck finally had decided to move on, he didn't get up and walk away. I could see where he actually had remained on his belly and crawled several yards before rising up and trotting off. Remember, this animal was, at most, two and a half years old!

Again, this disproves the theory that when making drives for big bucks, the more hunters employed the better. My belief is that, especially when driving big bucks, you're far better off with one or two very knowledgeable hunters trying to run those bucks past waiting guns.

Perhaps the most enjoyable aspect of making small drives is that I get to spend time hunting with some of my favorite people. As I said at the beginning of this chapter, so much of my deer hunting time is spent going solo. I spend so much time bowhunting from a cramped little tree stand that when gun deer season rolls around, I'm ready for a change of pace.

As I've revealed in this chapter, making small drives can be an effective technique for taking big white-tailed bucks with firearms. More than that though, it's an excuse to get together with good friends and do something we all love. As far as I'm concerned, it doesn't get much better than that.

# Chapter 13

# Pursuing Individual Bucks

If there were one chapter in this book that I would consider mandatory reading for every aspiring trophy whitetail hunter, this would be it. Insights gained from the following pages could well prevent a very costly mistake at some point during your deer hunting career.

Some current outdoor writers and self-titled white-tailed deer experts are greatly to blame for a major misunderstanding among hunters. You see, because of a concept passed along by these writers, many novice deer hunters wind up with the wrong ideas concerning hunting for trophy bucks.

Actually, I've been guilty of the sin myself. Many of the articles I've written for national magazines discuss at length the importance of figuring out the habits and travel patterns of an

*Experience has proven time and again that dedicating every minute of free time to one buck can be a costly mistake. This buck was just one of many I hunted during a recent season.*

individual buck. Many readers may have construed they should follow the techniques with just one buck, concentrating all their efforts on that one animal.

In reality, one of the costliest mistakes a deer hunter can make is singling out one buck and then dedicating his free time just to that deer. This mistake is most common among people who are just getting into the trophy hunting end of this sport, but I've seen even veteran hunters fall into the trap of hunting just one buck. In fact, I did this very thing during a recent season.

# A season wasted

The buck for which I had hung my hat was a massively antlered 10-pointer living in the big woods of northern Wisconsin. My obsession began the day I picked up a matched set of his shed antlers. Even with very conservative measurements, it appeared the monster deer would make the Boone & Crockett record book.

Over the summer I ate, slept and drank that big buck. Every day I spent at least some time thinking about him, devising strategies that just might prove effective. I often imagined how his mounted head would look on the wall of my trophy room.

The opening day of my state's archery season finally arrived. As you might expect, I headed for the woods where I knew the big "shed-horn buck" was living. I spent the entire day on my stand, but the only thing that ventured within range was a squirrel. I did see one deer — a doe — but she never got closer than 60 yards.

I spent every moment of free time that fall hunting the big shed-horn buck. Yes, I did come extremely close to being in the right place at the right time. In fact, one cold November morning, the monster deer stood a mere 15 yards from my tree stand. Unfortunately, a thick screen of underbrush prevented my getting a shot.

By the time archery season ended, I had hunted the buck to the point of exhaustion. Still, I was confident I could kill him during our nine-day gun season. So I mustered up a reserve of strength and put in a couple of grueling, all-day vigils on my tree stand. When I returned to my cabin on the evening of the second day, my brother Jeff was waiting with the news: someone else had shot *my* buck.

Now, it was bad enough the buck had been harvested. But even worse was that the fellow who shot the monster deer had no knowledge of the buck's existence until just seconds before he squeezed the trigger.

As far as I was concerned, my season was over. There was no other deer in that part of the state that could stimulate me to shrug off this disappointment and go on with my life. I took nearly a year to completely recover from the incident.

# Immaturity hunting maturity

I've brought this experience to your attention for two reasons. First, it demonstrates that *anybody*, even an experienced hunter, can get caught up in hunting for just one buck. And second, it shows that hunting one buck exclusively can cause a hunter to develop a very poor attitude regarding this sport.

It's true, I still spend a great deal of time each year trying to figure out the behavioral quirks and patterns of individual bucks. However, I no longer fall into the trap of limiting my energies to just one deer. Instead, I spread out my attention to include as many as a half-dozen (or more) mature animals.

Deciding which buck I'll hunt on a given day depends upon a number of circumstances. Conditions such as wind direction, pressure from other hunters and my own efforts have a tremendous bearing on my final decision. And buck size isn't always the deciding factor.

But regardless of warnings, thousands of deer hunters across the nation will single out one buck and then hunt that deer exclusively during some future season. My advice? Don't do it!

Of course, those prone to committing this error would argue that the more time they spend hunting one particular deer, the greater their chances for taking that deer. Not true.

This is because trophy white-tailed bucks, in most cases, are the most mature animals in a particular area. Being the most mature means they are, more than likely, the most cunning, wary and intelligent. Of course, this means they also are going to be the most difficult of all to harvest.

Unfortunately, many hunters who commit themselves to one deer have never tried taking a buck any older than two-and-a-half years of age. Hunters in this category simply haven't a clue about how to hunt super-reclusive, hyper-sensitive, mature white-tailed bucks.

# The case of the disappearing buck

To help illustrate the sort of trap many hunters fall into each year, allow me to paint a hypothetical situation. In this scenario, the hunter in question already has located a tremendous buck during a preseason scouting mission.

The man in our illustration is 20 years old and an aspiring trophy hunter. Although he has taken a few immature bucks in the past, he really hasn't spent much time hunting for mature animals. But as far as he's concerned, that doesn't matter. Everybody knows the most difficult thing about trying to kill a big buck is first finding such an animal. And he's already accomplished this task.

As many novice hunters, this guy figures that if he spends all his time hunting that one deer, the odds will eventually swing in his favor. So every time he's afforded even a small amount of time to hunt, he heads for the buck's home area. Little does he know that every time he trespasses the buck's domain, his chances for success actually decrease.

The young man initially is impressed with the amount of fresh *big* buck sign in and around the area where he first saw the big buck. However, as the season progresses, the less fresh sign he finds. And at the height of the pre-rut, when new rubs and scrapes should be appearing on a daily basis, he's finding absolutely no fresh buck sign at all. It's as if the big buck he was hunting suddenly has dropped off the face of the earth.

The buck this guy was hunting probably relocated. But I doubt seriously if he moved very far. The big deer probably moved just far enough so he could continue his daily routines, yet evade the young hunter. It's a very familiar pattern.

# The harder you hunt, the smarter he'll get

It doesn't matter how big an area you're hunting or how many different stand sites you've scattered about a buck's home range. If you spend every bit of your hunting time pursuing that one animal, there's an excellent chance he'll even-

*It really doesn't matter how many stands you have scattered about a buck's home core area. There's a strong chance that buck eventually will catch on to your presence if you spend all your time hunting him.*

tually figure out what's going on. From then on, you'll be doing nothing but educating that deer.

Throughout this book I've stressed the importance of not overhunting your stands and not spending a lot of time in one area. There's good reason for this. In my opinion, "burning out" a potentially good spot is one of the most damaging things a deer hunter can do.

I've actually seen it occur. Repeated human intrusion into a specific area during the course of one season has ruined the area for several seasons after. You stand a very good chance of having this happen if you limit your pursuits to just one buck.

## Keep your options open

At this point I can almost hear what you may be saying. If you ever find where a big buck is living, you'll hunt only that buck, but only when all conditions are absolutely right. I agree. It's the exact approach you should take whenever you're hunting mature whitetails.

However, when hunting one buck exclusively, waiting for the perfect conditions could mean going days or even weeks without hunting at all. Personally, I can't justify sitting home in front of the TV during hunting season just because the conditions are wrong to hunt one particular deer.

This is exactly why you should have several alternate bucks to hunt. Even though these deer may not create as much excitement in your life, they will give you an outlet for your energies on those days when you can't hunt your favorite area. Besides, you never know when a "bonus" buck may wander by one of your other stands.

The biggest reason many hunters decide to dedicate all their time to a single big buck is because these animals are becoming increasingly more difficult to locate. So once hunters learn the whereabouts of a tremendous white-tailed buck, many of them absolutely refuse to even look for any other big deer. In their opinion, doing so is just a waste of time and energy.

I find this way of thinking ridiculous! It's easy to dismiss the potential of any area simply by telling yourself no big deer live in that territory. Truth is, merely driving around in your car or sitting in a tavern talking about big bucks won't help you find one. You have to work at it.

*Once they pinpoint the exact location of a tremendous buck, many hunters refuse to look for other big bucks. This attitude gets them into trouble later on during the open season. You simply must have more than one option.*

I live in one of the most heavily hunted states in the upper Midwest. And contrary to what many people think, we don't have an extraordinarily high number of trophy-sized white-tails here in Wisconsin. In fact, we probably have fewer mature bucks than any of our bordering states. It's no easier for me to locate mature bucks than for hunters anywhere else. The reason my hunting partners and I are able to find so many big bucks every year is because we're constantly on the prowl for such animals.

I doubt seriously if the root of a hunter's problem is a lack of big bucks in some of the areas he's hunting. The way I see it, the problem for most hunters is that as soon as they find one big buck, they quit looking for others.

## Locating those big bucks

In case you're thinking that I can jump in my truck, drive a few minutes, and shoot a trophy buck, let me clear up that misconception. The many big bucks I hunt during a season don't live just a few miles from my house. Sometimes up to 130 miles separate the home core areas of some of those bucks.

But this is often the case with white-tailed deer. Once you raise your standards to the taking of mature bucks only, you've severely limited the number of target animals available. And I don't know of any small area in North America that has a large population of mature bucks running around. However, just about every area has at least a few deer of this caliber.

So, no matter where you live, I believe you have the option of hunting several different trophy bucks during the season. However, finding such animals may mean adopting an entirely new approach to the sport. To begin with, you'll have to range out a little further from home. Then you'll have to talk with lots of people; rural mail carriers, school bus drivers, farmers and ranchers, and even other hunters just might help you pinpoint a big buck or two.

In addition, keep in mind the bucks that got away. There's a world of difference between knowing where a big buck is living and actually harvesting that buck. This means there always will be those big deer you found, yet failed to kill. So if you take time to locate one or two mature bucks during the off-season, and then figure in the one(s) you failed to harvest in previous seasons, you should always be assured of having several different trophy bucks to hunt. (Many of the big bucks I'm currently hunting are "carry-overs" from other seasons.)

# Maintaining your "edge"

There are yet other negative factors associated with hunting for one buck. Constant failure, no matter what the sport, can be emotionally taxing. Also, hunting the same area and/or sitting the same stands day after day can become very boring and mundane. (Believe me, I've been there.) Either of these situations can cause you to lose that "edge" so vital when hunting for trophy whitetails.

Certainly, hunting a mature deer is never an easy task, and the energy needed to do it right eventually can cause a temporary letdown in your efforts. However, having the option of switching those efforts to different areas and different bucks may get you back on track and help reinstill that crucial "edge."

You still can dedicate more time to one buck in particular if you so desire, but don't get hung up on hunting that one deer to the exclusion of all others. I've even found that occasionally sitting on stands where I'm assured of seeing does, fawns and small bucks can be an ego booster and the exact therapy needed to deal with a whole string of "deerless" days.

You probably realize that merely discovering the home turf of a trophy buck doesn't guarantee you'll eventually score on that buck. This is because along with overcoming the keen survival abilities of the buck, you also may have other hunters to contend with.

Even if these other hunters are totally unaware of the buck's presence, it doesn't matter. Spending every bit of your time hunting a mature buck in an area that's also being pressured by others lowers your chances for success. This is yet another reason why it's important to have several different bucks to hunt.

To be honest, it does take tremendous self-control to limit your intrusions into the home range of a true stud-buck. But retaining this self-control should be a top priority throughout the season.

You may find this hard to believe, but I spend more time hunting bucks that score 125-140 than bucks that are sure candidates for the Boone & Crockett record book. The reason?

I'm convinced it takes far less pressure to drive the older, record book caliber deer into a strict survival pattern. Hence, it stands to reason that they should be hunted less frequently.

# Understanding your motives

It's my opinion that too many hunters these days harbor all the wrong reasons for wanting to kill a big deer. So what is it that drives some hunters to take up an exhausting pursuit of a big buck?

Over the past ten years, I've talked to a number of individuals who fall into this category. To them, harvesting a record-book buck is their number one obsession in life. But this obsession isn't fueled by love and respect for the animals they're pursuing. Rather, their efforts are spurred by a burning desire to see their names in lights and a quest for respect from their peers. As the rest of us know, that's *not* what this sport is about.

No doubt, you'll hear a story about a hunter who killed a tremendous buck after pursuing that animal exclusively for a long period of time. I don't deny that it can't be done. Quite honestly, I know of several instances where hunters shot mature bucks after spending every minute of free time pursuing that particular deer. However, such incidents are rare indeed.

In most cases, the hunters who took up those pursuits were unique individuals. They are a special breed — the most dedicated of all trophy whitetail hunters. These people are fully aware that their potential for failure is great, yet they accept this and press on. I'm afraid there are darned few of us willing to make those same sacrifices.

*Too many hunters harbor all the wrong reasons for wanting to kill a big buck. Rather than being fueled by love and respect for the animal, they are obsessed by a burning desire to see their name in lights. That's not what this sport is about!*

# Chapter 14

# Rub-Line Basics

Although I could cite a number of reasons why this chapter was my favorite to write, one stands out from all the others. Simply put, a thorough knowledge of rubs and rub-lines is the number one reason I've experienced so much success on mature white-tailed bucks over the years.

## The facts about rubs

Rub-lines are series of antler rubs found along the preferred travel routes of white-tailed bucks. Although very few rub-lines actually are laid out in a straight line, they almost always connect a definite point A with a very definite point B. Rub-lines are found along both the morning and evening travel routes of bucks.

Understand, first of all, that rubs are not made by bucks attempting to remove antler velvet. And it's a fact that rubs are far more than places where bucks have attempted to strength-

*A rub-line is a series of antler rubs found along the preferred travel route of a white-tailed buck. Although not on a straight line, the line does connect a definite point A with a definite point B.*

en their neck muscles.We've learned in recent years that antler rubs serve as both olfactory and visual signposts.

If you ever get the chance to watch a white-tailed buck making a rub, pay close attention to the entire ritual he follows. First, the buck will spend a bit of time smelling the rub-tree. He may even lick the tree. Next comes the actual rubbing sequence. Just how long or how aggressively the buck rubs depends upon several different factors, of which time of year seems most significant. Again, the closer to actual breeding, the more aggression will be displayed.

Watch closely and you'll notice that the buck may spend almost as much time rubbing his forehead against the tree as his antlers. Upon completion of the rubbing sequence, the buck will once again smell the rubbed area and perhaps lick the tree again. Then he's off on his travels.

The buck smelled the tree before rubbing to scent-check for signs of visitation by other bucks. If any other bucks had visited that particular rub-tree, his nose would have told him if it was a buck familiar to the area or a stranger. Rubbing his forehead against the tree and licking it enabled him to then leave his own scent behind.

# The key to hunting success

Although many different tactics and techniques can prove deadly for taking white-tailed bucks, it's my opinion that *none* is as consistently productive as hunting along active rub-lines. While many hunters may consider this a fairly bold statement, I assure you it is not made lightly. Thirty years in this sport have given me all the proof I need.

What makes hunting along active rub-lines such an effective tactic? In most cases, rub-lines are established by white-tailed bucks along those routes they feel most safe and secure using. With the exception of a couple weeks during the peak of the breeding period, bucks will travel along one or more of these rub-lines every single day of the open deer season.

Obviously, your job then is to figure out which rub-lines could prove most productive, which ones are being used by the biggest bucks in an area, and whether they are being used in morning or evening. Although these tasks may appear monumental, in reality they're not. By the time you finish reading this chapter, you'll be well-versed in how to accomplish each one.

# Patterning a buck

Before proceeding, it's important to explain what I mean by "patterning" a buck. This is because too many hunters get the wrong impression when someone like me talks about patterning a white-tailed buck.

These individuals think that patterning entails not only figuring out the exact location of a buck's most preferred travel route, but also figuring out exactly which day and at what time he moves along that particular route. My opinion? If it were that easy, there would be darned few white-tailed bucks left to hunt!

Successful patterning means simply that you've discovered *where* a buck might walk when he travels through a certain spot. However, figuring out exactly *when* he's going to walk through that spot is guesswork at best.

In 30 years of chasing white-tailed deer, I've seen only a handful of instances in which I almost could set my watch by the appearance of a big buck in a specific spot. (I might add these deer were living in areas that were totally unpressured.)

I've learned that the best I can do is figure out where a big buck prefers to walk when he travels about his range. And to this extent, finding and deciphering rub-lines is the most accurate and reliable way I've found to accomplish this task.

# Scouting rub-lines in the early fall

Many deer hunters still believe that the first flurry of rubbing in early fall is triggered by velvet removal. In actuality, that first flurry of rubbing actually indicates that velvet removal already has occurred. From that point forward, it becomes increasingly more easy to pattern the movements of a white-tailed buck.

The days of early fall are a time of relative leisure for the bucks. They spend the majority of their time resting and eating, so it stands to reason that most of their traveling will be between preferred bedding areas and prime food sources. Obviously then, this is where the most pronounced and frequently traveled rub-lines will be found.

Admittedly, finding active rub-lines during the very early part of the season can be quite difficult. Thick foliage and underbrush is one reason why this is so. In addition, after the

*Many hunters still believe that the first rubbing that occurs in early fall is triggered by velvet removal. Actually, the first flurry of rubbing is an indication that the velvet has already been removed.*

Once a white-tailed buck has removed the velvet from his antlers, not a day goes by that he doesn't rub his antlers on something. This rubbing increases in both frequency and intensity as the rut draws nearer.

initial post-velvet flurry of rubbing, white-tailed bucks seem to curtail their rubbing activities somewhat.

But although they've reduced the frequency, the bucks haven't quit rubbing altogether. Initially, it may appear the areas you're hunting are relatively "rub-free," but I doubt seriously if that is the case. Remember, once the velvet has been removed, not a day goes by that white-tailed bucks don't rub their antlers on something.

A very slow, deliberate approach works best when scouting for active rub-lines during the early fall. Thoroughly scouting the cover around the edges of feeding areas is a good way to start searching for fresh rubs.

Once you have found some sign of rub activity, scour the immediate area closely. Walk up and down the runways that enter or leave a prime feeding area to determine if the rubs you're finding are part of a "line" or merely random rubs.

If the rubs you're finding are on the sides of the trees facing the food source, then you've probably found the route used by the buck to return to his bedding area each morning. Conversely, if the rubs are on the side of the trees facing the bedding area, you've discovered an evening travel route.

To a hunter's benefit, antler rubbing dramatically increases, both in frequency and intensity, as fall advances. Of course, this increase in activity makes figuring out the preferred travel routes of white-tailed bucks progressively easier. By the time the late pre-rut period arrives, any woodlot that plays host to even a single white-tailed buck will show considerable rub activity.

## Scouting rub-lines in the spring

I've talked only briefly about locating rub-lines during the open season because I prefer to do most scouting for rub-lines during the spring. There are two reasons for this. First, at this time of year, visibility in the woods is better than any other time. Second, I don't have to be careful about where I walk during the spring.

I have no qualms about walking right through known buck bedding areas in the spring. In fact, I depend on spring scouting missions to pinpoint the exact location of preferred buck bedding areas. Following rub-lines back away from feeding areas is the most effective way I've found for doing this.

*The latter days of the pre-rut are the best time to hunt along active rub-lines. At this time of year, it's not unusual to see a trophy buck traveling along one of these corridors during broad daylight.*

My reason for being so gung-ho on locating buck bedding areas should, by now, be quite obvious. As I've mentioned so many times in this book, for a great part of the season, hunting success hinges directly on establishing stand sites in very close proximity to buck bedding areas.

Usually, I to start my search for rub-lines near known preferred food sources. Because white-tailed bucks show such an affinity for rubbing along the perimeter of feeding areas, I know this is the best place to concentrate my efforts.

For me, locating a single rub doesn't mean much. What I'm seeking is a series of rubs, on a definite line, heading back away from the food source. Once I've located such evidence, I strive to follow this rub-line all the way back to the buck's bedding area, keeping watch along the way for potential stand sites. These stands will eventually be used for morning hunts.

Once I've found the buck's bedding area, I work my way through the cover along the edge of his bedroom, as this is a preferred rubbing spot. I look for a line of rubs that extends from his bedding area toward a distant food source. Once it's been located, I follow this line of rubs all the way to the food source, once more looking for prospective stand sites along the way. These, of course, will be used for evening setups.

Where to set up along active rub-lines will be dictated largely by the time of year. Early in the season, you'll do best by locating your stands as close as possible to bedding areas. As the season progresses, however, you'll be able to set up closer to feeding areas. And during the final days of the pre-rut, you could score on a buck from a stand situated right on the very edge of a food source.

As I stated in an earlier chapter, waiting in ambush along rub-lines is least effective during the actual rutting period. However, setting up along active rub-lines becomes highly effective again when breeding is done and the bucks get into their post-rut patterns.

# The spring advantage

I'm sure some of you are wondering how locating rub-lines during the spring of the year can prove to be of any value during the following season. The answer is relatively simple.

To begin with, mature white-tailed bucks are notorious for establishing residency in a certain area and then, provided they are relatively unpressured, remaining in that area for the duration of their life. As long as food sources stay consistent, these bucks will use the same travel routes (rub-lines) year after year. And once you learn where his rub-lines are located, your chances of bagging a buck increase dramatically.

Even if you happen to locate the rub-lines of a tremendous buck during your spring scouting missions and then find out later that the buck had been killed during the preceding season, that's no reason to worry. There's an excellent chance another big buck will already have moved in and taken up residency in the former buck's core area.

More importantly, there's a better than average chance this "new" buck will travel along the same routes as his predecessor. Provided you've done your homework, your stand sites should already be in the perfect positions to take advantage of his patterns.

# How many rub-lines are enough?

Finding and then deciphering just a couple of rub-lines from a specific buck should in no way be considered an adequate scouting job. In fact, it's only a start. In most cases, I'll not rest until I've walked nearly every inch of a buck's home turf and located several different routes (rub-lines) he uses to travel about his range.

Sometimes this can be accomplished in just a couple of days. However, I've also taken many days — or even weeks — to pinpoint and then decipher the many rub-lines of a mature buck. To be sure, this can entail a *lot* of walking and a large amount of time. But knowing the location of several preferred travel routes of one buck will provide me with a number of options for hunting that deer.

Although it's entirely possible a white-tailed buck may have more than a dozen rub-lines established throughout his home range, there usually are a couple he prefers to use more than the others. These rub-lines are easily identifiable because they show much more rub activity.

# Rub-line size and frequency

The length of individual rub-lines can vary greatly from one buck to the next. For instance, I've seen examples of rub-lines that twisted and turned through nearly a mile of woods. On the other end of the spectrum, I've found rub-lines that were only 200 yards in length.

My years of research have shown that big woods bucks have a greater propensity for establishing long rub-lines than their farmland cousins. My opinion on this is that big woods deer, in general, are more nomadic and transient. They just seem more inclined to travel greater distances — for any reason.

The frequency with which bucks rub along their travel routes also varies from deer to deer. Some bucks seem to be rather "rub-crazy," marking out their lines of travel by making a rub every 20 yards or so. As you might imagine, it's a snap to locate and follow such a rub-line.

Of course, some bucks are just the opposite in nature. In such cases you'll find a rub every 200 yards — if you're lucky. These, of course, are the hardest of all rub-lines to locate and follow. From my observations, this seems to be common behavior for very mature bucks.

Other factors also can affect rubbing activity. One of the most obvious is the existing buck:doe ratio. Simply put, as the buck:doe ratio gets "tighter" in an area, you'll notice a definite increase in both frequency and intensity of the rubbing. If the ratio goes the other way, with does far outnumbering bucks, you'll see a decrease in rub activity.

Earlier, I mentioned that locating all the rub-lines of a mature buck sometimes can take days or even weeks. One reason for this is that as white-tailed bucks become older, they seem to spend less time rubbing.

Why they do this is still a cause for speculation. My guess is that as white-tailed bucks grow older, they become less preoccupied with breeding and more concerned with survival. (I guess they're a bit like humans in that regard.) Because of this, they rub less frequently and with less intensity.

## Buck size and rub size

It seems that each year, more and more hunters ask me about the buck size/rub size correlation. They all wonder if its possible to identify the size of a buck purely by the size of the trees he rubs.

For the most part, big bucks rub on big trees. And while it is true that small bucks occasionally will rub on large trees, I've found that they seldom initiate such rubs. Usually, rubs on large trees are first "opened up" by mature bucks. After this happens, every buck in the area may rub on that same tree.

For nearly 20 years I've used rub size as a guide for ensuring my pursuits are limited only to mature bucks. My rule of thumb is thus: *Any rub wrist-sized or larger in diameter denotes the work of a "keeper" buck.* Strict adherence to this rule has left me disappointed only a few times.

## Identifying bucks by their rubs

It's entirely possible to keep track of individual bucks purely through their rubs. For example, I've hunted bucks that preferred to rub on only certain species of trees. Some rubbed almost exclusively on poplar, some on pine and still others just loved to thrash tangles of red willow bushes.

It's also possible to keep track of individual bucks simply by the way they rub. I've pursued bucks who consistently rubbed very high on trees. As you might expect, I've also seen cases where bucks rubbed very low on trees. Certain antler characteristics may cause some bucks to leave behind very identifiable rubs. For example, non-typical or "sticker" points might be the reason a buck consistently makes scratches or gouges in strange places on his rub-trees.

Bucks with very heavy beading on their antler bases are bound to leave the bark on their rub-trees extremely frayed or frazzled. And scratches found far above the actual rubbed spot often indicates you're dealing with a long-tined buck.

Several years ago I spent a good deal of the season hunting a buck whose rubs were very easy to distinguish. This buck consistently picked on huge pine trees. He also apparently used only his brow tines to mark those trees.

## A rub-line success story

I harvested a dandy 10-point, 186-pound buck during a recent archery season in Wisconsin. I first located that deer by finding his rub-lines on a spring scouting trip in March. A quick spot-check of his core area during late September showed me the buck was just beginning to get "rub-active." After a bit of quick snooping I found and prepared a stand site for future use.

*It's sometimes possible to identify individual bucks purely by their rubs. For example, a certain antler characteristic, such as a "sticker" point, may cause a buck to leave scratches or gouges in strange places on his rub trees.*

*A combination of an aggressive rattling sequence and a stand placed along an active rub-line was the undoing of this big woods 10-pointer. I first located the deer's home turf while on a spring scouting mission.*

I waited until late afternoon of October 24 before returning to hunt the area. Not long after settling into my stand, I heard a deer approaching. Several minutes later, a big buck stepped out of a nearby alder thicket. He was making his way along an active rub-line that passed within 20 yards of my stand.

The 10-pointer eventually walked right by my position, affording me a relatively easy bow shot. I waited a few minutes after the fatally hit deer crashed out of sight before climbing down and taking up his trail. I found him lying dead only 50 yards away.

Although the above success story pertains to a specific deer, it could be changed only slightly and applied to many of the trophy bucks I've taken over the years.

As I stated at the beginning of this chapter, a thorough knowledge of rubs and rub-lines is the number one reason I've experienced so much success on mature whitetails. If there's a tactic more effective for taking big bucks than waiting in ambush along active rub-lines, I'm not aware of it.

# Chapter 15

# Scrapes: Fact And Fiction

I'm sure many long-time deer hunters will agree that no aspect of white-tailed deer behavior has received more ink over the past 20 years than scrapes. But in my opinion, no other aspect has suffered from more misinformation. Unfortunately, this printed misinformation has played significantly in hunters' lack of success.

The biggest reason for my concern is that much of this misinformation has been passed along by supposedly reliable sources, i.e., scientists and biologists. Hunters thus have been led to believe that everything they've read and heard about scrapes is gospel.

From the day I started planning this book, I intended this chapter to appear last. It's last, not because the information is less important than that in other chapters, but because the information might just be the most beneficial of all.

I also want to clarify that this chapter was not written to downplay the effectiveness of scrape hunting. Setting up near active scrape-lines can be very productive during the latter stages of the pre-rut. The purpose of this chapter, instead, is to enlighten white-tailed deer hunters about the truths regarding scrapes.

If you don't already know about scrapes, they are places where pre-rut white-tailed bucks have pawed away leaves and other debris from a forest floor. (Bucks usually will paw until they expose the dirt.) In most cases, a scrape will be located directly beneath an overhanging branch.

There is no standard size for a scrape. I've seen many that were only a foot in diameter. However, I've also seen scrapes ten feet wide. In fact, my friend Dave Hartman recently showed me photos of a scrape he'd found which measured over 20 feet in diameter. But regardless of the size, shape or location, scrapes all serve the same function.

# The myths of whitetail scrapes

In order to better understand the truths of scrape hunting, it's important to first discuss some of the untruths read and heard over the years. As I relate these untruths, you probably will realize that you have, indeed, seen the majority of this stuff in print at one time or another.

According to many scientific findings, white-tailed bucks begin establishing their scrapes during the early pre-rut period. I fully agree with this conclusion. However, from this point forward, my personal findings are very different from those of the scientific community.

Some biologists and outdoor scientists would have us believe that white-tailed bucks establish the majority of their scrapes in spots where they know does are spending a lot of time. Supposedly, this is done so that during the pre-rut period, the does will find one or more of these scrapes. They'll then note the exact location and file away this information for use at a later date. But the theory gets far more complicated.

Of course, the bucks are checking their scrapes on a daily basis. And by the time the late pre-rut period rolls around, they know exactly which scrapes the does are visiting most frequently. They then concentrate the majority of their attention on these, their "primary" breeding scrapes. (I'll deal with

Over the years, hunters have been led to believe that scrapes play a large role in the breeding ritual of white-tailed deer. I insist that nothing could be further from the truth.

the fallacies of this primary and secondary scrape stuff a bit later.)

At the first hint that she may be coming into estrus, a white-tailed doe immediately searches out the nearest "primary" scrape. Upon arriving at the scrape, the doe may spend a bit of time pawing in the dirt. Next, she urinates directly in the scrape. Then she moves off a short distance and waits patiently for her suitor to come along.

Eventually, the dominant buck in the area will show up to check the scrape. Immediately, he detects an odor that sets his brain on fire. In no time at all, he tracks down the "hot" doe. After a short chase, the doe stands and allows the buck to mount her.

The buck then stays with the doe until her estrus cycle is finished. At that time, he heads back to his scrape-lines to check for other potential girlfriends. When he finds one, the above-described chain of events is repeated.

Even I have to admit, this is a cute, romantic little scenario! Too bad it's filled with such an abundance of misinformation.

# What scrapes <u>really</u> mean

Contrary to what we may have been told about scrapes in the past, they are *not* a buck-doe thing. In fact, buck-doe interaction at scrapes is very rare. As for scrapes having some important function in the actual breeding ritual, that's the biggest piece of misinformation of all!

The truth of the matter is that scrapes are a buck thing - plain and simple. Scrapes are not established by bucks so they can keep tabs on the local doe population. Rather, scrapes enable bucks to keep very close track of other buck activity throughout their home ranges.

The best way I know to describe this phenomena is by paralleling scrapes to dog behavior. Let's say you live in a neighborhood where three of your neighbors own male dogs. One day, all three of these dogs are running loose — but they are not running in a pack. Rather, each of the free-roaming dogs is cruising different parts of the neighborhood alone.

As you sit in your house and look out a window that faces the back yard, one of the male dogs runs across your yard, goes right to a certain bush, smells the bush, then lifts his leg and urinates on that bush. He then runs off to resume his reconnaissance of the neighborhood.

A short time later, a second male dog runs through your backyard. This dog also ends up at that "certain" bush. He smells the bush, then lifts his leg and urinates on it, just as the first male dog did. Just as quickly, he's gone.

Before you have time to turn and walk away, the third male dog trots into view. As the two dogs before him, this one eventually stops at that one particular bush then goes through the same sniffing, leg-lifting ritual as his two predecessors.

By first smelling the bush, each of the dogs was able to determine which dogs, if any, had been there before. Urinating on the bush then enabled each to leave behind his own scent-filled calling card.

Because each of the three dogs recognized the scent of dog(s) which already had visited the bush, there probably were no confrontations. However, things would have been quite different if somewhere along the line a strange dog had visited that bush and left behind his scent. In that case, each of the resident neighborhood dogs would have searched out this intruder. After catching up to him, they would have set a few things straight regarding the local pecking order.

## Scrapes mark territory

Okay, so what does the behavior of dogs have to do with white-tailed bucks and the way they relate to their scrapes? Quite a bit actually.

As I stated earlier, white-tailed bucks begin laying out and running their scrapes during the early pre-rut period. However, where these scrapes are located has very little to do with the local antlerless herd. However, scrape location has a lot more to do with the way bucks travel about and relate to certain things within their home ranges.

Even minimal investigation will show that the majority of a buck's scrapes usually are located along travel routes that link his preferred bedding and feeding areas. Most likely, you'll find he also has established a number of scrapes along the perimeters of his most preferred feeding areas.

As the dogs in my earlier scenario, every time a buck uses a certain travel route or visits a particular food source, he checks and freshens his scrapes in that area. For the most part, his routine is the same on each visit.

First, the buck will sniff the scrape, then the overhanging branch. Next, he'll lick the branch and rub the end of it direct-

*All the bucks living in a specific area, from the smallest to the largest, may spend time working the same scrapes. The only time a confrontation will occur is when a strange buck slips into that area and works one of the scrapes.*

ly into his preorbital gland. The buck will then spend a bit of time pawing at the scrape. Finally, he'll step into the scrape, hold his hind legs together and urinate. The urine will run down onto his hock glands before dribbling into the freshly worked dirt of the scrape.

Licking and rubbing the overhanging branch into his preorbital gland and urinating into the scrape enables each buck visiting that scrape to leave behind his particular scent in two different places. More importantly, though, by sniffing the scrape and the overhanging branch, a buck can verify if any other antlered animals (not antlerless deer) have visited the scrape before him.

All of the bucks living within one core area, from the smallest to the largest, may check and freshen any of the scrapes found in that area. This is common behavior and doesn't really produce a cause for confrontation amongst those bucks.

However, if a buck from somewhere outside that core area happens to wander in and work one of those scrapes, that's a completely different matter. Just as the dogs might, the resident bucks will immediately detect the odor of the strange buck. The first order of business, then, will be to track down this intruder and teach him a few things about the local caste system.

Scrapes, in other words, are a way for white-tailed bucks to mark both their travel routes and the boundaries of their core areas. Routinely checking these scrapes enables bucks to keep track of all the antlered activity in these areas.

And how about all those theories concerning primary and secondary breeding scrapes? While these theories enhance the romantic, biological "buck-meets-doe" image of scrapes, I'm afraid they're just more misinformation.

# Why some scrapes are larger than others

Some scrapes are much larger than others because they are visited more often. On that point I agree with the scientists. However, I don't agree with the popular explanation for why these scrapes are visited more often — that they're located in areas of heavy doe concentrations. I'm convinced this frequency of visitation occurs solely because the scrape just happens to lie on a travel route used more than other routes.

It only stands to reason. The more times a buck walks along a certain runway, the more times he'll work the scrapes found on that runway. By the end of the pre-rut period, some of these scrapes may have the diameter of a kitchen table.

A large number of bucks living in a relatively small area can also cause some scrapes to grow considerably larger than others. Several years ago, my brother Jeff videotaped a bachelor group of 16 bucks. A dozen of these animals possessed racks large enough to qualify for the Pope & Young record book. I'm sure you can easily imagine the size to which some of the scrapes in that area grew by late pre-rut.

# A little logic and common sense

For those who disagree with my findings regarding scrapes, permit me one question: If scrapes really play an active role in the breeding ritual of white-tailed deer, then why do bucks completely abandon their scrapes when breeding begins?

That's right. I said bucks completely abandon their scrapes once the actual breeding begins. If theories about scrapes as meeting places for breeding bucks and receptive does were true, then scrape activity should reach its peak during the rut. In actuality, just the opposite occurs.

If you haven't yet spent enough time in the woods to substantiate this, I suggest you talk to a few of the more experienced deer hunters from your area. I'm sure they'll confirm that, once the rut starts, scrapes go cold.

As further support for my theory regarding scrapes, consider this. Let's say — according to popular theory — that a white-tailed buck discovers a receptive doe has visited one of his scrapes. He takes up the doe's trail, eventually catches up with her, and then spends the next 24-36 hours with this doe.

By the time the doe's estrus cycle ends, the buck may have been led a mile or more from his home core area. Now, if the common theory is true, the buck will travel all the way back to his home range and once again start running his scrapes. Sooner or later, another hot doe will show up at one of these scrapes. Then the breeding ritual starts again. What a bunch of venison baloney!

A bit of common sense quickly reveals the inaccuracy of this belief. If white-tailed bucks truly did act in the above described manner, a huge number of does would go unbred ev-

*An estrus doe may lead a breeding buck miles away from his home range. Once finished with this doe, that buck certainly isn't going to waste time and energy traveling all the way back to his home area to start running his scrapes again.*

*Once the rut kicks into gear, breeding bucks go right from one receptive doe to the next. Scrape-lines and rub-lines are completely abandoned at this time.*

ery year. Simply put, the bucks would spend more time traveling and freshening scrapes than breeding.

In reality, once the rut kicks into gear, white-tailed bucks go right from one hot doe to the next. They find these hot does by cross-checking doe/fawn runways, by cruising through the woods with their noses into the wind, and also periodically walking through doe/fawn bedding areas. Believe me, they *don't* find does by checking scrapes.

If this be true, waiting in ambush along active rub- and scrape-lines is the least effective method to employ during the hectic days of peak rut. (For suggestions as to what tactics and techniques are most productive at this time, refer back to the chapter titled, "Hunting The Rut".)

# The evidence of experience

I've spent thousands of hours in the woods during my 30 years of hunting white-tailed deer. Along with being a fairly good hunter, I've always seen myself as a first-class observer — when in the woods I pay very close attention to everything that goes on around me.

Those many hours of personal observation have pointed out some very notable facts. First, it's obvious antlerless deer do all they can to avoid any close contact with big bucks. So saying, they'll avoid those areas that harbor the most big buck activity. This becomes increasingly evident as the rut draws near.

On some occasions I've seen does and fawns completely bypass areas of especially heavy scrape activity. If the purpose of scrapes were to provide bucks with a way of meeting prospective mates, then antlerless deer literally should flock to these special "meeting places." Rather, they display quite the opposite behavior.

The second fact about scrapes I've observed is that, just as with rubbing, white-tailed bucks seem to spend less time scraping as they grow older. Although older bucks initially open up most scrapes, the more aggressive, younger bucks are responsible for enlarging and doing the most digging at those scrapes.

Time and again I've sat and watched immature, second- and third-year bucks tear apart existing scrapes. They paw with great enthusiasm, throwing dirt and leaves several yards behind them — grunting loudly all the while.

*During the past five years, I've noticed that truly big bucks spend very little time actually scraping. However, they spend a great deal of time scent-marking "licking branches."*

On the other hand, my observations have shown that very mature bucks scrape very little, if at all. This does not mean, however, that older age class bucks don't spend any time marking their territories. They thoroughly mark their travel routes and home range boundaries, but with rubs and the licking of branches.

Over the past five years, I've paid close attention to the licking branch phenomenon. I've often seen a big buck approach a licking branch, then spend a short time mouthing it and rubbing one or both of his preorbital glands on the very tip of the branch. Before leaving, the buck urinates onto his hocks. *None* of these big deer has made even the slightest attempt at actual scraping.

Waiting in ambush near one of these licking branches can be a very productive pre-rut tactic. But the obvious question that arises is, "If big bucks don't scrape in conjunction with licking branches, how on earth do I go about finding them?"

Unfortunately, witnessing a buck working a licking branch is the only way of determining where one is located. But while this may sound like quite a task, it really isn't. The key is to remember that big bucks establish licking branches along the routes where they feel most secure. And these are exactly the same places where you'll find active rub-lines.

The majority of licking branches I've pinpointed were found as I waited in ambush near an active rub-line. While the bucks I saw on those days didn't come close enough for a shot, they did provide me with information that has since proved valuable.

You may argue that because my findings about scrapes can't be documented by file upon file of meticulous data, there's no way they can be considered accurate or valid. All I can say to these people is *all* the information found in this book was compiled by a very experienced, highly-observant and aggressive white-tailed deer hunter. I believe that's what matters most to other serious hunters.

**DEER & DEER HUNTING:** *A Hunter's Guide to Deer Behavior & Hunting Techniques*
Al Hofacker, Editor
Al Hofacker, founder and former editor of the popular Deer & Deer Hunting magazine, combines his outdoor experience with his editor's quill to bring you one of the finest deer hunting guides available.
*$34.95, Hardcover, 8-1/2"x11", 208 pp., 100 color photos*

**1995 DEER HUNTERS' ALMANAC**
Staff of Deer & Deer Hunting Magazine
A great way to start the season, the new 1995 edition is loaded with helpful facts, forecasts, ballistic data and hunting tips. It makes a perfect hunting companion.
*$6.95, Softcover, 5-1/4"x8-1/4", 208 pp., 50+ b&w photos*

**301 VENISON RECIPES:** *The Ultimate Deer Hunter's Cookbook*
Staff of DEER & DEER HUNTING Magazine
If you need to feed a hungry bunch at deer camp, or serve special guests in your home, look no further for creative ways to prepare hearty and delicious venison.
*$10.95, Comb-bound, 6"x9", 128 pp.*

**ADVANCED WHITETAIL DETAILS**
Staff of DEER & DEER HUNTING Magazine
This reference includes the first-ever transparent overlays of white-tailed deer anatomy! As a comprehensive yet easy-to-read handbook, it answers the technical questions most often asked by experienced deer hunters.
*$14.95, Spiral-bound, 8-1/2"x11", 24 pp., 50+ photos/charts*

**1995 WHITETAIL CALENDAR**
The seventh edition of our Whitetail Calendar contains 12 full-color photos even more stunning than those featured in previous years. The DEER & DEER HUNTING Whitetail Calendar is perfect for home, office or your hunting cabin.
*$7.95, Unfolds to 2-1/8"x16-3/4"*